S0-ALK-136

DISCARDED FROM
GARFIELD COUNTY
LIBRARIES

Brought to you
by the passage of
ballot measure 6A
in 2019.

THANK YOU
Voters!

Garfield County Libraries
Carbondale Branch Library
320 Sopris Avenue
Carbondale, CO 81623
(970) 963-2889 Fax (970)-963-8573
www.GCPLD.org

Praise for Dr. Tamer Seckin and Endometriosis

"[Seckin] writes with compassion, repeatedly assuring women that their symptoms are real and deserved of appropriate, effective treatment. He explains the disease and its impacts, and in clear language includes case studies of patients who have recovered under his care."
– Library Journal

"There is hope, and there is treatment… *The Doctor Will See You Now* is a good place to start your road to recovery."
– Padma Lakshmi, Co-founder Endometriosis Foundation of America

"One of the biggest issues surrounding Endometriosis is the lack of awareness. It is important for female and male teens to be educated on this disease because females are at risk for multiple health complications the longer their case of endometriosis goes undiagnosed. Males should also be educated on this disease because their mothers, daughters, wives, and other loved ones can also be affected. Just like women, men can also help spread awareness."
—Lexie Stevenson, actress *The Young and the Restless*

"Now young women have the opportunity to learn the symptoms early on. Perhaps they can be spared from long term suffering and possible infertility. Mothers, please listen to your daughters. Daughters talk to your mothers or a trusted adult. Together find the right doctor who will listen to you."
—Diana Falzone, Journalist and Women's Health Advocate

"One of the best endometriosis surgeons is Dr. Tamer Seckin, a premier gynecologist specializing in endometriosis. Throughout my practice and teaching career, I have personally observed numerous top surgeons, both in Europe and North America, performing difficult endometriosis surgery in their operating rooms and, without hesitation, I can recommend Dr. Seckin as one of the best of the best."
—C.Y. Liu, MD, Past President, American Association of Gynecologic Laparoscopists (AAGL)

"Dr. Seckin blends his knowledge and surgical skills with compassion and understanding of patient concerns. His many years of hands on experience and patient interaction combine to make this book a very worthwhile read."
—Harry Reich, MD, Pioneer in the field of laparoscopic surgery

"In this moving and informative book, Dr. Seckin provides an important resource for women with endometriosis - a common, widely misunderstood, and understudied condition…Targeted research can lead to earlier diagnosis, improved treatments, and eventually, preventative care to put an end to Endo."
—Peter K. Gregersen, MD, Professor of Molecular Medicine, Hofstra-Northwell School of Medicine

Endometriosis

Endometriosis

A GUIDEBOOK
FOR
GIRLS

By Tamer Seckin, MD

TURNER PUBLISHING COMPANY

Turner Publishing Company
Nashville, Tennessee
www.turnerpublishing.com

Copyright © 2019 Dr. Tamer Seckin. All Rights Reserved

Endometriosis: A Guide for Girls

No part of this publication may be reproduced, stored in a retrieval system, or transmitted in any form or by any means, electronic, mechanical, photocopying, recording, scanning, or otherwise, except as permitted under Sections 107 or 108 of the 1976 United States Copyright Act, without either the prior written permission of the Publisher, or authorization through payment of the appropriate per-copy fee to the Copyright Clearance Center, 222 Rosewood Drive, Danvers, MA 01923, (978) 750-8400, fax (978) 750-4744. Requests to the Publisher for permission should be addressed to Turner Publishing Company, 4507 Charlotte Avenue, Suite 100, Nashville, Tennessee, (615) 255-2665, fax (615) 255-5081, E-mail: submissions@turnerpublishing.com.

Limit of Liability/Disclaimer of Warranty: While the publisher and the author have used their best efforts in preparing this book, they make no representations or warranties with respect to the accuracy or completeness of the contents of this book and specifically disclaim any implied warranties of merchantability or fitness for a particular purpose. No warranty may be created or extended by sales representatives or written sales materials. The advice and strategies contained herein may not be suitable for your situation. You should consult with a professional where appropriate. Neither the publisher nor the author shall be liable for any loss of profit or any other commercial damages, including but not limited to special, incidental, consequential, or other damages.

Cover design: Jenny Carrow
Book design: Tim Holtz

Library of Congress Cataloging-in-Publication Data

Names: Seckin, Tamer, author.
Title: Endometriosis : a guide for girls / by Tamer Seckin, MD.
Description: Nashville : Turner Publishing Company, [2020] | Audience: Ages
    13-18 | Summary: "This book will be the only comprehensive and
    accessible guide for young women and girls who are or may be struggling
    with the physical, psychological, and social effects of endometriosis"--
    Provided by publisher.
Identifiers: LCCN 2019027341 | ISBN 9781684423651 (paperback) | ISBN
    9781684423668 (hardcover) | ISBN 9781684423675 (ebook)
Subjects: LCSH: Endometriosis--Juvenile literature.
Classification: LCC RG483.E53 S432 2020 | DDC 618.100835/2--dc23
LC record available at https://lccn.loc.gov/2019027341

9781684423651 Paperback
9781684423668 Hardcover
9781684423675 Ebook

Printed in the United States of America
17 18 19 20 10 9 8 7 6 5 4 3 2 1

Table of Contents

To the young women who are affected by endometriosis, you can find the answers you need and seek the health you deserve. Your pain is real and treatable, and your courage is unparalleled.

Foreword

I've been a fashion model in New York City for about four years, since I was twenty-two years old. I come from a family of movie and television entertainers who date back several decades, so I guess you could say I'm comfortable in front of the camera. I'm into that whole social media thing, mostly because I have to be. Instagram has become a second portfolio for many models, and always being "out there" comes with the territory.

One day last spring, lying in bed exhausted, bloated, cramping, and helpless, I was passing the time by scrolling through my Instagram feed, which was filled with photos of other models. While it is part of my job to follow people like this, I realized that following beautiful, thin women was not exactly great for my current emotional state. I was growing weary of the perfection that Instagram users had chosen to portray. I was tired of the fake, curated, aesthetically pleasing and perfect lives that I had to look at every single day, especially on days when pain was plaguing me. Though my own posts occasionally portrayed a similar lifestyle, that was not the reality at all. Most of the time I was at home in sweatpants cooking with my husband, hanging out with my family and lifelong friends, taking college courses . . . and popping Vicodin every four hours to stop me from shrieking, having to use heating pads on my belly and back, and going down an endless spiral of depression.

This is the real me, and this is endometriosis.

I decided that I couldn't live a lie anymore. I couldn't have young girls look at me the same way that I was looking at those "perfect" models' profiles. While I had contemplated getting rid of Instagram altogether, I wanted instead to use my voice and my truth to send a real message to girls out there. I was going to be honest, open, and real with my struggles so that other girls might not feel so alone.

So, I rolled out of bed and crawled into the bathroom, phone in hand. I was wearing plaid pajama pants and a sports bra. I turned sideways, took a photo of my bloated stomach, and posted it.

"This is not a pregnancy announcement," I wrote in the caption. "This is what some of us in the endo community like to call 'endo belly.'" I spoke about my views on the deceptive ideals that the modeling industry portrays, and I told my followers to please feel open and message me if they had endo. I promised I would be an ear to listen.

Within minutes, I had more than a hundred messages in my inbox.

Many girls said they were in pain, desperate for any help or advice. Many girls were about to go into their second, or eleventh, laparoscopic excision surgery. Many girls were in middle school getting their first period. And many women were mothers with children of their own. This disease crossed all barriers, regardless of age, weight, economic background, language, and country. Women messaged me from Paris, from Milan, from all over the world. As far apart as we were, and as different as we could be as people, we all had that one connection. We all knew each other, understood each other, and loved each other immediately. We knew the exact pain that the other was going through. We had a bond that no other woman could understand unless she, too, had endo.

Regardless of our cultural differences and the stage of the disease, I felt more connected to these women and girls than most other people I knew, because these women and girls knew firsthand my pain and my struggle. While my endometriosis story is not nearly as bad as others', I have had my share of the bottomless black hole of this disease, just as all who share their stories in this book have.

I did not experience any endometriosis symptoms until I was in my early twenties, and my life was instantly flipped upside down. I was always the laid-back free spirit, the fun girl with loads of energy who never complained. But, very quickly, I became the antithesis of that. Suddenly, I was spending thousands of dollars on doctors, specialists, naturopaths, vitamins, acupuncture. My energy dwindled, and even the most mundane of tasks was difficult to perform. I canceled plans with my friends, events with my family, and dates with my husband. This soon became my normal. Doctors couldn't find answers, and I was told to just go on birth control. I felt like I was losing friends and becoming a burden to everyone around me, which led to depression and a diagnosis of pre-menstrual dysphoric disorder. Add that to a previous diagnosis of polycystic ovary syndrome, along with a daily schedule of taking metformin to regulate my insulin levels.

What was the scariest part of all this?

I felt like I was losing myself.

I felt like my old body was gone, and my new one had been overtaken by a demon.

I was very fortunate to have been diagnosed early in my journey. I found Dr. Seckin through my sister-in-law who, at the time, was dealing with endometriosis as well. After one appointment with Dr. Seckin, I felt heard. After three appointments with Dr. Seckin, I was scheduled for surgery because my pain was increasing rapidly. While no endometriosis showed up on any scans, it was found during surgery, and it was everywhere. Dr. Seckin removed multiple lesions and diagnosed me with stage II endometriosis. What most people don't understand is that this disease never leaves you. It's chronic, which is why I still have difficult and dark days. But overall, since my surgery, I'm living a much more positive life, taking each day as it comes.

After the success of his first book, *The Doctor Will See You Now: Recognizing and Treating Endometriosis*, Dr. Seckin makes this second book even more compelling and real. It's not just the simple and understanding way he explains all of the complications of this disease but the brutally honest stories from other endometriosis survivors. Sharing their experiences loud and clear, these strong women give you every ounce of personal insight that can help you help yourself. They are heroes to me, and I believe they will soon be heroes to you.

Since the day I posted that picture last spring, I told myself that no matter where my career takes me or where I end up in life, I will always be an open ear or helping hand to any other girl with endometriosis. Being a part of this book is an extension of that. Don't ever hesitate to reach out on Instagram, and use the knowledge and advice in this book to get yourself well, no matter how difficult it is or how long it takes. Then join me and the rest of the endo army of women worldwide by speaking out and helping others to get well. We women need to come together and lift each other up. Having endo means we're forever a part of a sisterhood, and together we will find a cure.

With love,
Alaia Baldwin Aronow

Introduction

I know the ceaseless pain that endometriosis inflicts upon every phase of your life. It forces you to miss school or work, to quit sports or dance, to give up on starting or maintaining relationships. It tries to convince you that you're "crazy" by turning family, friends, and even doctors against you, and by creating feelings of anxiety, depression, and isolation.

In essence, it tortures your body, mind, and soul until you've lost all hope.

Endometriosis will usually make its presence known in your last few years of elementary school, middle school, or early high school, and often during your first menstrual period, if not sooner. It will likely cause debilitating pain in your pelvic region and heavy blood flow, before spreading to other parts of your body.

Because endometriosis is not a household name like cancer or diabetes, and because doctors *still* aren't required to learn about it in medical school, it takes an average of twelve years to diagnose. That means most teenagers who have it suffer into at least their mid-twenties or early thirties before they have any clue what torments them. They are repeatedly undiagnosed or misdiagnosed—ignorantly told that the pain is in their minds, that it is part of becoming a woman, or that it's the result of some other disease or condition.

"Endo," as it is commonly called, affects an estimated 176 million females of childbearing age worldwide, including one in every ten in the United States. That means, statistically, if you have three hundred girls in your school, thirty of you will have it. And yet, it's likely that you don't know about a single one of their cases, because it may be difficult for many girls to talk about their periods, especially if they're painful. And if someone *is* willing to talk about it, who will listen and take her seriously?

That's why endo is referred to as the silent epidemic. Girls have been suffering in silence not just for decades or centuries; there are documented ancient medical writings about the disease that are more than four thousand years old. Yet today, there are still many stigmas and taboos associated with menstruation that we must dismantle. Together, we must continue to educate the public and medical professionals alike to put an end to the silence that surrounds your pain.

For the past forty years, it has been my mission to bring awareness to and ultimately treat this disease. I have successfully performed surgery on more than three thousand patients using the unique laparoscopic deep-excision method, which is the closest thing we have to a cure. It may be exactly what you need too. But, as you'll read, surgery isn't always the best first option for young girls. Through proper management (nutrition, exercise, certain medications, and other methods), it may be possible to combat the effects of endo early on with limited disruptions to your education, job, and social relationships, and without jeopardizing your ability to one day have children.

Over the course of this book, you will read stories from several of the most courageous young women I've ever had the pleasure of knowing, many of them in their teens or early twenties, along with some of the people closest to them who have witnessed their struggles. They will all speak directly to you about their endometriosis journeys so that you know without a sliver of doubt that your concerns about your body and the pain you are feeling are genuine, that you are not in this predicament alone, and that you, too, can conquer this beast.

In between their stories I will explain what endometriosis is, remedies for you to try and to avoid, and how to control the psychological and social effects of the disease. One of the most difficult aspects of having endometriosis is feeling like nobody believes that your pain is authentic or as severe as you say. This book will fully arm you with the truth and knowledge about the disease so that you can overcome your fears and confidently stand up for yourself. If your cry for help has been dismissed by your doctor, parents, siblings, teachers, coaches, school nurse, employer, friends, or romantic partners, you will be able to educate them so that they believe you and can fully support you in your quest for healing.

In 2018, my foundation, the Endometriosis Foundation of America, presented an award to Grammy-nominated singer and songwriter Halsey, who bravely had gone public on Twitter about her fight against endometriosis. She said in part of her tweet: "With doctors essentially telling me I was being a big baby about my period . . . finding out that I had endo was the most bittersweet moment because it meant I wasn't crazy! I wasn't a 'baby'! I had every right to be feeling like the world was caving in."

Like Halsey and everyone else with endo, you have that same right. You also have the right to be well, to be pain-free, and to live the way you want to live. I'm here to give you hope. What matters most is the voice of an informed young woman being honest about her pain. With the support of family members, empathetic friends, and conscientious doctors who listen to and believe you, you can catch and treat this disease at its infancy. I believe that your pursuit of a new and happy life can begin now.

Endometriosis

To defend yourself against endometriosis, you first must understand what it is and what it isn't. You have to be able to recognize its symptoms, know the damage it can impose upon your body, and realize that medical doctors frequently lack basic knowledge about it. More than half the battle is education. Once you know about this disease, your journey toward healing can begin.

CHAPTER 1

What Is Endometriosis?

There are two key aspects about endometriosis I want you to understand before I explain specifics about the disease.

The first is that not one single girl anywhere in the world is immune to it. If you're doubled over in pain or have other symptoms of the disease, that doesn't necessarily mean you have it, but you very well might. Don't ever discount it as a possibility just because of your impeccable health history, race, nationality, or "good genes," or because someone claims that you're too young to have it or that the pain is in your head.

Dilara, like many of the young women you'll read about, started feeling symptoms when she was twelve. Eight years later, at the age of twenty, she still hadn't been diagnosed with endo.

"There came a point when I felt like I was dying every day," Dilara said. "One day I went to urgent care because I was throwing up everything, and they sent me to the emergency room because I was about to go into shock from all of the water loss. I was in the ER for ten hours. They took blood, did an ultrasound, conducted all kinds of other tests, and they still couldn't figure out what was wrong. When one of the doctors mentioned endo as a possibility, they concluded that I was too young for it and that it was probably some cysts. So, they sent me home."

As you may know from personal experience, and as you'll continue to read, ludicrous conclusions like that by doctors are quite typical.

The second aspect about endo I want you to understand is that it's a chronic disease with no cure. That means no matter what you do to try to treat it, whether it's as complex as having it removed through laparoscopic deep-excision surgery or as fundamental as changing your diet, it could return someday. But don't be discouraged. Whatever treatments you undergo should enable you to effectively reclaim your life and manage the disease instead of the disease managing you. The effort toward discovering a cure is ongoing—I'm personally part of this mission—but it's going to take many more years of research before one is found.

Now, let's get into the nitty-gritty of endo and what it can do to your body. Once you understand the science behind the disease, you will know more about endo than most adults, including doctors who spent years in medical school. That's no joke. And with that new knowledge will come empowerment, and with that empowerment will come confidence, which you will need in order to be heard and properly cared for.

The uterus, also called the womb, is an organ with thick walls in the middle of your pelvic region where a fetus grows until it's ready to be born. Why would I define something that you may think every girl already knows? Because not everyone does. Not every girl has been educated at home or in school about her body, which is an enormous obstacle we face when trying to bring awareness to the disease. There may also be dads reading this who, though they may not admit it, could use a lesson in the female anatomy.

What is endometriosis?

It is when endometrium-like tissue is present *outside* of the uterine cavity. The uterine cavity is the space inside the uterus that runs from the two fallopian tubes at the top to the cervical canal at the bottom.

At the top of each side of the uterine cavity is a fallopian tube, and each of the two tubes is connected to an ovary. The ovaries release eggs each month, in a process known as ovulation, which travel through the fallopian tubes and into the uterus during a girl's menstrual cycle (which I will discuss in detail in chapter 2). At the bottom of the uterus is the cervical canal, a narrow passageway that connects the uterus to the vagina. The vagina connects to the outside of the body and allows a female to have intercourse, give birth, and menstruate. Menstruation is the body's natural monthly process of discharging blood and other material from the lining of the uterus.

When I stated that endometriosis is "endometrium-like tissue" present *outside* of the uterine cavity, I was referring to tissue that resembles the endometrium, which is the *interior* lining of the uterus that grows every month to prepare the uterus for the implantation of a fertilized egg. What makes that tissue on the outside "endometrium-like" instead of the endometrium is just that: it's outside of the uterine cavity instead of inside, where it should be. So, the tissue lining the uterus inside the cavity is the endometrium. If that tissue erroneously makes its way outside of the cavity, it becomes endometriosis.

What causes endometriosis?

We know, through recent studies, that it can be present at birth. There are experts who believe that every girl is born with it, but that it only activates in some of them, and not until their first menstrual period. Some believe, as I do, that endo is genetic. If your mother had it, your chances of having it increase. If you *and* your mother had it, your daughter's chances of getting it increase even more. I also believe in the widely accepted theory that endo is caused by retrograde menstruation. In other words, a girl's menstrual blood flows back into her body during her period instead of completely out of her body like it should.

Fourteen days after a girl's body ovulates (when the ovaries discharge eggs through the fallopian tubes and to the uterus), if the eggs have not been fertilized by a sperm—meaning there is no pregnancy—the girl will have her menstrual period. During her period, the endometrium naturally sheds. If the menstrual flow of blood properly discharges from her body, the flow will carry the endometrium with it through the cervix (the opening at the bottom of the uterus that connects to the vagina). However, if the menstrual flow does not discharge as it should, it may leak back into her body. That blood with the endometrium tissue initiates an inflammatory process, creating new implants in areas outside of the uterus. And that's when the problems begin.

The body's immune system, sensing that the tissue is not where it's supposed to be, will try to eliminate it. That bout between the immune system and the misplaced tissue will result in inflammation and scar tissue.

As a girl's hormones (estrogen and progesterone) naturally fluctuate during her menstrual cycle, the inflamed tissue will respond to those fluctuations by growing. In other words, estrogen and progesterone serve as food for that tissue. If that tissue were on the inside of the uterus where it should be, this hormonal action would be perfectly fine. But since the tissue is on the outside, it's growing in areas where it shouldn't be growing. And because there is no natural way for it to exit the body, it grows and grows and grows as it's being fed. *This* is endometriosis—menstrual periods that are literally stuck inside of a girl's body, like leeches.

The endo can grow deep and wide, spreading and clinging to the appendix, rectum, ovaries, intestines, leg nerves, outside of the uterus, and in some rare cases the diaphragm, lungs, kidneys, or brain. This can lead to adhesions, scarring, internal bleeding, bowel or urinary dysfunction, constipation, painful intercourse, and infertility. The overall physical pain can be unbearable and usually leads to deep psychological pain.

When you endure that much physical and mental trauma, you may find your mental health being tested. You may lose your ability to attend school or to keep up with your career, your friends, your family, or your significant other. The disease, through no choice of your own, becomes your identity and negatively rules every phase of your being. This is how much control endo has.

You can see why it is so important that it be caught and treated early, and why it is so important that *endometriosis* becomes a household word like *cancer* or *diabetes*. It is shocking that one in ten women in this country has endo, yet you have been told by people who should be helping you that your pain and symptoms are normal. You may have been taught by society that talking openly about your periods is taboo. You may have been labeled as a dramatic attention-seeker. These attitudes force you to try to hide your anguish and live a normal life under abnormal circumstances, which is impossible.

Trust me when I say this disease is as real and powerful as the pain you are feeling, and though you may just now be hearing the word *endometriosis* for the first time, you are far from alone.

My Name Is Lexie

"They thought I was making all of this up."

I got my first period when I was eleven. I remember it well because the cramps were insanely painful, and they would worsen with each month. When I went to see my pediatrician about it, she said it was nothing unusual for a girl my age to experience. She gave me some pain medication and sent me on my way.

When the meds didn't help, my mom took me to another doctor who diagnosed me with acid reflux. I changed my diet to try to calm it down, and it initially helped a little, but it didn't solve the problem. The pain gradually increased over the next four or five years, reaching its worst one night when I was at a high school party.

I was fifteen or sixteen, and the party was at a friend's house. There were no parents but plenty of alcohol. I had had just a couple of drinks when, suddenly, a razor-sharp pain shot through my stomach. I screamed, fell to the ground, and instantly curled into a fetal position. I wasn't drunk, and this wasn't a nauseous feeling. It felt more like I'd been stabbed with a knife. Luckily, the foreign exchange student whom my family had been hosting, along with a couple of his friends, were nearby and drove over to pick me up—literally. They had to carry me to the car and up to my bedroom when we got home. I bawled my eyes out all night; the pain did not relent until morning.

When I went to the doctor the next day, she said, "Well, this definitely isn't acid reflux, but I really don't know what it is." I would find out a few years later that, privately, my mom suggested to that doctor and to others we saw that I might have endo. My mom had the disease, and she knew the symptoms. But all of the doctors said that wasn't possible because I was too young. Mom never brought it up in front of me because, admittedly, I'm a hypochondriac. No matter what she would have suggested I had, I would have claimed to have had it. Of course, that might have helped me in this case since I would have been insisting that I had endo, but I'd cried wolf so many times in the past that the doctors' opinions would have likely trumped mine.

As time went on, the pain strengthened and became a daily occurrence. I struggled to get through a school day, if I could make it to school at all. I became a regular visitor to the ER where some of the staff got to know me by name. One time they said my pain was probably caused by appendicitis. It wasn't. Another time they said I was constipated. I wasn't. They were so perplexed that they finally asked my parents, "Is Lexie getting enough attention at home?"

They thought I was making all of this up.

I was a pretty good actress for my age, but to pull that off would have been award-winning. When my dad scoffed at that question, doctors filled me up with morphine and narcotics; they didn't know what else to do. It was another bandage to an obviously serious problem that nobody could figure out.

A year later, when I was seventeen, I had another major attack. Again, I was away from home, this time at my then boyfriend's house. You know that pain at the party that I said felt like I'd been stabbed with a knife? This was worse. It felt like the knife had a jagged edge and was being twisted. My boyfriend's parents drove me to meet my parents halfway, and then I proceeded with my mom and dad to the hospital. When we got there, nurses gave me what they said should have been enough morphine to calm me down and even knock me out, but it didn't. I was still wide awake and screaming for all of the hospital to hear.

The doctor did an ultrasound while my mom, again in private, told her that she thought I might have endo. She was the first doctor since all of this started when I was eleven years old to agree with my mom. The ultrasound showed three ruptured cysts and a growth on one of my ovaries. I was sent to another hospital where they did more tests and eventually scheduled surgery. Once I was opened up, they found endo everywhere. The surgery lasted eight hours, with a bulk of that time spent removing part of one of my intestines that was entangled in endo.

When I turned eighteen, with no major attacks since the surgery and feeling better than I'd felt in a long time, I moved from the East Coast to the West Coast to try to start a career in acting and singing, my lifelong dream. I was able to get an audition with the long-running daytime soap opera *The Young and the Restless,* and I was hired to play the role of Mattie Ashby. I was nervous because I knew that endo could affect my job, but the producers, cast, and crew couldn't have been more supportive when I told them about it. Any time I feel the endo flaring up, which still happens on occasion given that it's a chronic disease, they treat me like a queen. They get me a chair, a hot pack, and my medication, and they stop shooting my scenes until I'm ready. It would obviously be better for everyone if this didn't happen, but when it does they have my back. It's the kind of support that every girl with endo needs but isn't always fortunate enough to receive.

My periods still aren't the best in the world, but they're nothing I can't handle. I've learned through experimentation that gluten and dairy cause inflammation in me, so I avoid those, and I'm especially careful about what I eat when I know I'm about to go to an audition. I also try to schedule my auditions around my periods, just to be safe.

You're going to be learning a lot about this disease as you continue reading, and you will receive fantastic advice from some amazing young women. I think the best advice I can offer, which I know all of these women and Dr. Seckin will agree with, is to never accept an answer from anyone if you believe it's not the right answer for you. So many endo patients are misdiagnosed or provided temporary fixes by doctors, just like I was. They're accused by medical professionals or even their own family and friends of exaggerating their pain. As a result, they suffer needlessly for years.

It doesn't have to be that way for you. It shouldn't be that way for you.

Learn from those of us who have been through this. You know your body better than anyone. Trust what you feel and fight for yourself until you receive the treatment you deserve. And know that I and the millions of others with endo are with you every step of the way.

CHAPTER 2

Painful Periods Are Not Normal

I will discuss numerous symptoms of endo in the next chapter, but a painful period deserves a chapter of its own. The pain often starts with your first period, and it will likely be the most agonizing pain of your young life. I call it the first cardinal symptom of endo.

Talking openly about your period is generally taboo in America and in other countries. American schools don't educate students enough about a woman's menstrual cycle. Girls learn most of the basics of how to "deal" with menstruation from a mother or sister or friend, and boys are rarely part of the discussion. This lack of education may make it intimidating for you to have a meaningful conversation about your period with anybody. As a result, you may try to hide the symptoms of this natural occurrence—symptoms that, if abnormal, could be early signs that you have endo. Your silence, which is absolutely understandable given the taboo surrounding menstruation, feeds this epidemic, which is one reason it takes an average of nearly twelve years to diagnose the disease.

Boys should be taught about girls' periods not only so they understand a woman's anatomy and biology but also out of respect for what girls go through each month. If boys don't have that knowledge, there is little chance of them ever knowing about endo, which means they will never be part of the solution.

You should be taught prior to reaching puberty when you can expect to get your first period, what will happen to your body when you do, and how to physically and emotionally handle it in the moment. Having your first period when you don't know what is happening to you, or having your first period occur at school during class instead of at home, can be traumatizing. You shouldn't have to learn about it for the first time as it's happening.

You should be invited to ask questions by your mother, sister, guardian, pediatrician, gynecologist, school nurse, or even the men in your life—be it a father or doctor—and you should be able to get the answers you need without fear of embarrassment. I have two daughters, and given what I do for a living, it was easy for me to discuss this with them when they were young. But I certainly don't expect it to be that easy for every man. I recommend that a significant female adult, someone you trust, be the one to discuss this with you. Not because a man can't or shouldn't, but because, as is the case in nearly all situations, the best education and empathy will come from those who have the most knowledge and personal experience. And nearly every woman knows about periods.

Whoever the adult is imparting this wisdom upon you should be proactive about it and not wait for you to come to them. They should observe and note your behavior, attitude, and physiological changes. They should pay attention to how you are doing in school and extracurricular activities and to how your relationships are with your friends. Has anything changed for the worse without any obvious explanation? If so, you should be approached with tenderness and love, as your period is presumably the most notable physical and hormonal change you've experienced thus far.

Why am I telling *you* all of this? So that if you haven't received any assistance from the adults around you, you can share my words with them. I would also hope that when you are older and if you have young girls in your life—a daughter, a niece, a daughter's friend who needs help—you will remember this and step up for them.

You will usually get your first period anytime between the ages of eight and fourteen. The average age in the United States is twelve. If you have gotten your first period before eight or have not gotten it by the age of fourteen, you should consult your pediatrician or a gynecologist. Your period will follow general signs of puberty, such as a spurt in your height, growth of pubic hair, or growth of underarm hair. You could also have some light abdominal pain or light cramps in the months prior. These changes in your body are due to the powerful effect of the female hormone estrogen (this same hormone is also responsible for fueling the inflammatory process associated with endometriosis). Eventually, blood will discharge from your vagina. That is the signal that your period has started.

A normal menstrual cycle lasts twenty-eight days, though it is considered "normal" if from the first day of your current period to the start of your next period is between twenty-four and thirty-eight days. Some women know the day and time their period will start every month. If yours differs each month, that's okay, as long as it falls within that range.

Your menstrual cycle is the monthly process your body goes through to prepare for pregnancy. It doesn't mean your body senses that you are trying to get pregnant or that you are having intercourse. It's simply the way the female body evolved—to prepare for pregnancy every month. During this process, the lining in your uterus—the endometrium—builds and thickens while, at the same time, levels of the hormones estrogen and progesterone rise. If there is no pregnancy, those hormone levels drop, which is a signal to your body to begin your period. That's when the endometrium lining sheds and, along with blood, passes through your cervix and out your vagina. As your uterus contracts to expel that tissue, it causes cramps, a normal symptom of having your period.

But there is a *huge* difference between cramps and abnormal, crippling pain.

It's normal for most girls having their periods to feel cramps and some discomfort. It's not normal when that pain has you doubled over to the point that you can't get out of bed or walk. It's not normal when the pain is so intense that you are vomiting or it hurts to have a bowel movement. It's not normal when you can't go to school or work because you physically cannot get there and function. This is when adults need to listen to you and believe you. Telling you to "suck it up" or that "it's part of womanhood" is insulting and scientifically incorrect. It's why many girls with this disease seek isolation and try to suppress their pain. If you have endo, an extended delay in addressing your pain could allow the disease to grow and spread throughout your body. That could lead to more complications as you get older, including infertility.

Eva had intense pain with her first period at the age of twelve.

"Every time I would go to the doctor about it, they'd say, 'Eva, you're fine. This is what happens to girls. You have to get through it,'" she said. "It reached a point where I was going to the emergency room almost every month, and the same thing would happen each time: they'd run tests, say they couldn't find anything wrong, declare it to be normal period cramps, tell me to take Motrin, and send me home. When I would insist it was more than that, they'd say that maybe it was gas or bloating, but in any case they couldn't do much for me. Sometimes they'd call me 'crazy' for saying I was in so much pain, as if I were making it up. Finally, my mom stopped taking me because we knew they weren't going to do anything. It felt hopeless."

I'll later discuss when you should speak up about the pain you're feeling. If your period has caused you some uneasiness, you shouldn't dash out the door with my book to a doctor and insist that you have endo. However, you shouldn't feel pain, whether it's during your first period or your two hundredth period, that literally forces you off your feet and prevents you from being able to live your life. Get to your doctor if it's unbearable, and openly discuss with him or her the possibility of endo. If the doctor dismisses your concern without any tests or a referral to a gynecologist or specialist, or if he or she seems to have less knowledge about endo than you do, find another doctor.

Advocacy for you starts with you. Don't rely solely on others to take care of you, and don't be silent because others have shrugged you off. Keep fighting until your voice is heard.

My Name Is Dilara

"I was supposed to somehow magically
know everything and manage it."

Dr. Seckin says that girls with pain or other symptoms of endo are often dismissed or ridiculed by friends, family members, or doctors—not necessarily because those people are mean or uncaring, but because they lack education about endo.

I am proof of his words.

You read in the first chapter about how I felt like I was dying every day. What made it a million times worse was the absence of any support from those around me.

I got my first period in sixth grade; I was twelve years old. It was accompanied with significant pain and bleeding. Though I'd never had a period before, I sensed it was more than what "normal" should be. I approached a few of my girlfriends to ask them how a period was supposed to work. They couldn't believe I would ask such a personal question. I continued talking about it anyway, telling them what my period was like, hoping to draw any advice out of them that I could.

"You're being weak," one of them said to me.

"Don't be so spoiled and think this only happens to you!" another snapped.

"You're obviously trying to get attention," a third girl claimed. "We all have it, and you don't hear us complaining."

And those were my closest friends.

I later said something about my condition to a few female family members and their friends who were much older than me, hoping that they could impart some wisdom. By this time, regular vomiting with my period had become a thing.

"Vomiting? Oh, honey, that's normal," one of them said as the others nodded in agreement. "You just have to deal with it."

The symptoms worsened with time. By high school, nausea and fatigue were daily occurrences. The length of my period had extended considerably. I had no more than ten to fourteen days between the end of one period and the start of the next. I missed a lot of school because the symptoms, always attacking me in unison, were too much to bear. But I was such a good student with exceptional grades that nobody questioned my absences. When I did make it to classes, I'd take tests squatting in my desk chair or curled up on the floor. Again, nobody asked why or seemed to care.

I was an athlete, specifically a kickboxer and swimmer. Some days I hurt so much that I couldn't compete. I once told my female swim coach that I needed to sit out a meet; I explained why, but she wouldn't listen.

"You don't understand," I cried. "I can't move!"

"Just swim!" she ordered. "We all have it!"

I was in biology class one day when we happened to be studying hormones and cycles. I asked my teacher after class if he could help me.

"I have my period all the time, and it's killing me," I said.

"Uhhhhhh . . ." He was mystified and visibly uneasy. Yes, a biology teacher.

"I . . . don't . . . know," he stuttered. "Maybe talk to your mom?"

Talking to my mom never worked. It's not that she didn't care; it's that in her culture a period was never talked about. She's from Turkey, which is also where I grew up. Female reproductive health is not talked about anywhere in the world like it should be, and Turkey is even more silent about it. I was never told as a young girl what to expect from my body. I was never told I should go to a gynecologist. I was supposed to somehow magically know everything and manage it.

New symptoms continued to surface, including diarrhea, constipation, and passing out routinely from the pain. I'd lost thirty-five pounds in about six months, yet everyone around me still insisted this was normal.

Maybe I'm as weak as they say I am, I wondered. *Maybe I'm exaggerating.* What happens to so many girls with this disease was happening to me: I was beginning to believe others and doubt my reality.

I was twenty when I finally dragged myself to a gynecologist for the first time, someone I found on my own online. She did a sonogram and said that I had endometriosis. I'd never heard the word before. Despite her diagnosis, there were some things about her demeanor that made me uncomfortable, so I made note of the word *endometriosis* and took it to another gynecologist. She was an older woman who I thought would know what to do. During my examination she reached inside me and held my ovary, which I would later find out was covered in endo. I screamed in pain.

"Owwww!" I howled.

"Oh, stop being so dramatic!" she barked. "You need to have a higher threshold of pain!"

I cried. I couldn't believe this was how I was being treated.

I left her office distraught, but I refused to give up. I couldn't. The state my body was in wouldn't allow me to. I did more research online and found Dr. Seckin, who determined during our first meeting that I needed surgery immediately.

But what would this outrageous story be without one final parting shot at me?

As I was being wheeled on a gurney toward the operating room for my surgery, screaming in distress at a decibel level so high that patients on other floors probably heard me, a nurse was walking next to me. She wasn't part of Dr. Seckin's team, just a general nurse with the hospital.

"Are you having a lot of pain?" she asked.

I glared at her before letting out another wail that echoed through the hospital halls.

"Don't worry," she said. "My daughter has the same thing. She passes out in school all the time. It will get better when you have a kid."

Really. That's what she said.

My surgery was a success, and I'm a new person today. But this story isn't about the surgery itself. I want you to know that there will be a lot of ignorant people around you when you try to seek help for what you are feeling, and there is no avoiding them. Not because they're cruel; they just don't know. But do not let them get to you. Do not let them convince you that you are being weak or dramatic or seeking attention. Believe in yourself and what you're feeling, then vigorously pursue whatever means necessary to get better. There really are people who will listen to you and help you. Unfortunately, you likely won't find them until you've gone through the ignorant ones first. I hope that knowing that little nugget, which I didn't know at your age, will put you on a path toward finding the right people much sooner and being properly treated much quicker.

CHAPTER 3

And Then There Are These Symptoms

Like some other diseases, the severity of your endometriosis is classified into four stages: I (minimal), II (mild), III (moderate), and IV (severe). All stages can be treated in some way. However, the earlier the disease is diagnosed, the better you will likely feel in the long run.

The classification of your endo is not determined by the pain or any other symptom. It is determined by, among other things, the location of the disease and how much it has spread. So, you could have stage IV endo and feel hardly any symptoms. Or, you could have stage I endo and be seriously hurting. I mention this for two reasons.

First, if you have a lot of symptoms or are being crippled by one in particular, don't assume that it's too late to do something about it or that irreparable damage has been done to your body. You could still be in the early stages, which is what an endo specialist can determine.

Second, if you aren't having many symptoms or if they don't start until later in life, it doesn't mean that you should ignore them or think that you'll have time to "get to them later." When you feel your body is doing *anything* out of the ordinary, it's trying to tell you something. Listen to it.

Ileana fit that second reason perfectly. She had only one symptom: a painful period, which caused a shooting pain through her abdomen. What was uncharacteristic about it was that it didn't start until she was twenty-two years old. Within four months of her feeling it, I did emergency surgery to remove large chocolate cysts (cysts filled with fragments of endometrial tissue, thickened blood, and inflammatory enzymes that can cause extreme pain), along with her endo-covered appendix and endo from her diaphragm muscle. Any time endo reaches as high as the diaphragm, which is near the rib cage, it can be especially dangerous.

"When I was a teen, I never had the debilitating pain that a lot of girls with endo have during their periods," Ileana said. "I didn't miss school. I didn't miss my swim meets. My periods weren't super painful. I could take an Advil or Tylenol and go about my day. It wasn't until that first shooting pain that I knew something was wrong.

"You can have severe symptoms and mild endo or, like me, you can have mild symptoms and severe endo," Ileana continued. "I was in complete shock when I was told how much it had spread. I think I was fortunate to not have the many symptoms that a lot of girls have when they are young teenagers, but I was also lucky that I paid attention to that pain the moment I felt it, considering how much endo was eventually found."

Aside from painful periods, symptoms of endo that you may experience include abdominal queasiness, nausea, vomiting, diarrhea, heavy bleeding, killer cramps, painful sex, painful bowel movements, neuropathy, miscarriages, infertility, and fatigue.

Abdominal queasiness, nausea, vomiting, and diarrhea could occur prior to your first period. Heavy bleeding could begin as soon as you have your first period. Yes, some of these five symptoms could be indications of other issues and not endo. Maybe you have the flu or ate spoiled food. You want to be careful not to jump to the conclusion that you have endo (something I will discuss a bit later). For right now, however, know that these are some of the early symptoms of endo, and you'll need to pay attention to them if they persist, especially during your period.

Killer cramps, the second cardinal symptom after painful periods, are cramps that are well beyond a nuisance or inconvenience. They would force you to miss school, work, athletics, or social activities. They are also usually accompanied with a heavy and prolonged menstruation with clotted blood. If killer cramps sound similar to painful periods, there is certainly a correlation. I separate them because painful periods can include much more, such as pain shooting throughout the pelvic region and into the legs. Also, while killer cramps will normally happen during your period, they can also happen during ovulation—when eggs are released from the ovaries in the middle of the menstrual cycle (about two weeks before a woman's next period).

Painful sex is the third cardinal symptom. You may not be sexually active now, but if you are at some point, be aware that if the disease is on your vagina and rectum, those two organs could be adhered to each other and cause heightened pain during intercourse.

Amanda had been having painful periods since sixth grade. In high school, she'd been dating a guy for a year when they tried to have sex for the first time.

"It was an absolute disaster," she said. "When I explained to him how much pain I was in, he was very compassionate about it." When she had sex with someone else in college, with her endo still undiagnosed, the pain was much of the same, but she became weary of having to explain it. "I thought that's how sex was going to be," Amanda said. "A lot of times I kept quiet and just tried to get through it."

A woman who is experiencing pain during intercourse often will not say so to her partner for fear of rejection or interrupting intimacy. And she may not bring it up to her doctor unless asked because sex may not be easy for many people to discuss, especially when it's causing problems. This is another obstacle we have to overcome to bring awareness to this disease.

A painful bowel movement is the fourth cardinal symptom. We've all had laborious bowel movements at one time or another, maybe because of what we ate or how much we ate. But bowel movements for someone with endo, especially during her period, can cause severe pain. In my first book, I talked about a patient who had bowel movements so painful she said, "It literally felt like my insides were being cut with razor blades as the feces moved through." Nobody should ever have to tolerate such pain.

The fifth cardinal symptom is neuropathy, which is pain caused by damaged nerves. When you have neuropathy, endo attacks the nerves directly or indirectly. An example of an indirect attack would be scar tissue that was created by endo pulling on a nerve. An example of a direct attack would be the endo latching onto a nerve itself. The pain from neuropathy that is caused by endo will ordinarily be felt in your back, leg (the sciatica nerve), or crotch area. Like all symptoms, neuropathy by itself is not necessarily a sign that you have endo, but if you have fierce leg pain that coincides with your period or a painful bowel movement, the possibility of endo is something to consider.

Miscarriages, sadly, are not uncommon for those who have endo. Some of my older patients have had multiple miscarriages. The good news is that many of those patients, after having the endo properly removed, were able to have children. The link between endo and miscarriages is not yet fully understood, but recent studies have shown there is definitely a connection.

Endo is also a leading cause of infertility. The disease does not directly cause infertility, but endometriosis patients could struggle to bear a child. The presence of endo can prevent the fertilization process between sperm and egg, it can distort a woman's pelvic anatomy and cause the fallopian tubes to become blocked, or it could cause ovaries to fail to ovulate.

Anna had had endo symptoms since her period started at the age of fourteen. She and her husband started to try to have children when she was twenty-seven after having two laser surgeries, as well as taking various medications, which did little to minimize the damage from all those years of endo. Through natural and various artificial methods over the course of several years, they were unsuccessful. That's when she came to see me.

"I thought Dr. Seckin would do a quick clean up, but that wasn't the case at all," Anna said. "Not only was I filled with scar tissue from the laser surgeries I'd had, he removed forty-six lesions, including forty-one that tested positive for endo. It was plastered and splattered everywhere, including on my urethra, colon, and rectum."

I also diagnosed Anna with diaphragmatic endo, which I removed in a second surgery four months later. She is healing now, and I will be meeting with her and a fertility specialist soon. Though she is thirty-four today, the surgery has given her hope. Not all of my patients are able to bear children after surgery, but most of them can.

What frustrates Anna is that she knew for years she had endo. She watched her mother endure it and struggle with fertility as a result. But the short-term fixes doctors provided Anna, along with her resilient nature, fooled her into thinking that it wasn't devastating her body as much as it was. Unfortunately, the endo never stopped growing and spreading.

"It's all about education," Anna said. "I knew I had it, but I didn't think it could be that destructive. I truly didn't understand the impact it could have on my life, the impact beyond the physical pain. Everyone needs to know the ability of this disease and what it can do to you down the line."

Fatigue is another symptom that can be caused by many things other than endo, which is why it would have to occur with one or more other symptoms, such as a painful period or killer cramps, for endo to be considered. Fatigue means you are physically exhausted, completely void of any energy, and for no apparent reason. If endo is causing your fatigue, it's because your body is trying to eliminate the disease. It's a violent war inside you between the endo and your immune system. You may not know that it's happening as it's happening, but you will definitely feel the fallout from it.

The final symptom is genetics. It may sound odd to call genetics a symptom, but it essentially is. Researchers are hoping to identify a genetic link to endo that may one day lead us to a nonsurgical cure. Until then, the fact remains that if your mother or sister had endo, you are six times more likely to have it. If you have any of the symptoms of endo, you should talk to the women in your family to see if they ever had them, or if they know if they had endo. Remember, many people didn't (and still don't) know what the disease is. Their painful periods or killer cramps or painful bowel movements from years ago may have been ignored by their mothers, doctors, or others, forcing those women to live through the pain without proper treatment. Knowing your family's health history, as I will address in the next section, can be vital to detecting and treating various diseases in their early stages. Women should add endo to that list.

Symptoms can be tricky. If you have a sore throat, it could be caused by strep or simply by the dry air. If you hurt your foot playing soccer, the injury could be as severe as a fracture or as mild as a sprain. If you have painful periods and fatigue, you could have endo or you could have something else. But with a sore throat you will get a strep test to know for sure. With an injured foot you will get an X-ray to know for sure. In the same vein, with endo symptoms, you need to know for sure. Don't let doctors tell you that you don't have it just because they don't *think* you do. Make them prove it. Until they do, it has to remain on the table as a possibility.

My Name Is Emily

*"It's never too early to seek help,
even if you're eleven like I was."*

I was a pretty normal kid growing up, but things began to change when I was eleven years old and started feeling killer cramps. I didn't know what was causing them, though, because I hadn't had my first period yet. Of course, I've since learned that cramps that occur before you start menstruating could be a symptom of endo. When I finally did get my first period at the age of thirteen and noticed that the cramps occurred at the same time, I thought, "Okay, that's what this has been all about the past two years. It's just part of becoming a woman." So, I rolled with it the best I could. Unfortunately, other symptoms would continue to pop up and make my life miserable.

From the ages of about thirteen to fifteen, I passed out five times. Each time I was told by a doctor that it was probably from dehydration, so I drank more water and pushed forward. Also during this stretch my immune system had become very weak. Whatever anyone around me had, be it a cold, flu, or some other ailment, I could count on catching it no matter what preventive measures I took.

I was involved in multiple sports in middle school and high school, such as soccer, tennis, and skiing, but the two sports I loved the most were horseback riding and field hockey. I was a decent athlete, loved to compete, and gave it all I had in every practice and competition. But around the age of sixteen, I noticed my skills had begun to diminish because of all the symptoms.

While the cramps had lingered, I also had a lot of nausea and dizziness, issues with my bowel and bladder, and fatigue. When I was nineteen it was excruciatingly painful to use the bathroom. Those daily symptoms and my inability to perform to my expectations on the field also created a lot of emotional grief. I was put on various medications, none of which did much of anything.

The fatigue was especially difficult to overcome. I struggled just to climb onto my horse. In field hockey we had two-a-day practices during the summer, and I could barely make it through one. What puzzled me the most was that I was getting as much as ten hours of sleep some nights, and yet when I'd wake up, I'd be so exhausted that I couldn't move. People would say, "Well, you know, you're a growing girl, and this is part of that." My rebuttal was, "Yeah, but there are plenty of girls my age who are growing girls, yet they are successfully competing at high levels." Nobody had a response to that.

This was my life for ten years, until Dr. Seckin finally diagnosed me with endo when I was twenty-one. Through surgery, I had it removed from my bladder, bowel, right ovary, and pelvic wall. My appendix was also taken out. Since then, I no longer have the nausea, extreme fatigue, or immune issues. I feel some of the cramps that I've had since I was eleven, but to a much lesser degree. I'm also on birth control pills, which have alleviated a lot of the pain (Dr. Seckin will explain how a little later). Overall, my quality of life has improved dramatically. Any issues I have today are totally manageable.

If you can relate to any or all of the symptoms I had or any other symptoms that endo can thrust upon a girl, I want you to ask yourself one question: "Can I physically do the things that other people my age can do?" If you can't, then something is wrong, and you should not stop asking questions until you figure out what it is. I don't mean that you need to be at the same skill or academic level as everyone else; we are all different in those respects. I'm saying that if you can't even give the effort toward a sport or class or job because you are constantly in pain, sick, or out of energy, that's not normal. I got into a funk that had me wondering if the reason I couldn't compete at a high level was that the other girls were better at sports. I knew deep down that wasn't the case, but this disease will try to make you question yourself. Don't let it.

No question is a bad question to ask. If you're not getting help from your doctors or anyone else around you, explore online for information about endo. Stories from people like me are not only in this book but are all over the internet. Find some that resonate with you and your symptoms, then take your arsenal to your parents and to a new doctor until your voice is heard.

One more thing: it's never too early to seek help, even if you're eleven like I was. Despite all of my symptoms, it took ten years for me to be diagnosed. Don't let that happen to you.

CHAPTER 4

When Your Doctor
May Be Wrong

Based on what you've read thus far, do you think you might have endometriosis? You probably have a good idea whether you might, but you don't know for certain.

An endo expert can tell you with near certainty if you have endo based on a clinical exam and testing, such as a sonogram or MRI. However, you also need to have the lesions identified as endo through laparoscopic surgery and confirmed as endo under a microscope by a pathologist. Only after those four steps will you know with 100 percent certainty if you have it. But you should have some idea, based on your symptoms and what I have shared with you about the disease, whether endo is a possibility.

Unfortunately, because many primary care doctors and gynecologists know so little about endo, it's often not on their minds as a possible diagnosis. That's why the vast majority of my patients who see me for the first time come with a long list of misdiagnoses they've received, such as irritable bowel syndrome or appendicitis. As you've read and will continue to read from those endo patients sharing their stories, when a misdiagnosis occurs, it can create a slew of other issues: continued growth of the endo, an increase in pain, useless and sometimes dangerous medications prescribed, the possibility of one or more unnecessary surgeries, and depression. I believe that no diagnosis is better than a misdiagnosis. At least with no diagnosis, you still have a clean slate and can immediately continue investigating the cause of your ailments. A misdiagnosis steers you in the wrong direction and gives you the false belief that you're on a path toward wellness.

Irritable bowel syndrome, or IBS, is one of the most common misdiagnoses. It's a disorder that affects the colon and has endo-like symptoms, including diarrhea, constipation, bloating, cramping, and abdominal pain. IBS can generally be fixed with medication or a change in diet; surgery is rarely needed. Doctors mistake endo for IBS because they know all about IBS symptoms and nothing about endo symptoms. Their hearts are in the right place, but their knowledge is limited.

A doctor checking for IBS, normally a gastroenterologist, will scope your mouth, esophagus, stomach, rectum, and colon. Unless the physician spots something out of the ordinary, such as the potential for cancer, he or she will usually diagnose you with IBS because they don't know what else it could be. Most patients will accept such a diagnosis because the doctor is doing all of that scoping and he or she is the expert, right? But, as you now know, scoping the insides of those organs will not reveal the endo, because endo would be on the *outside* of the organs.

"I was diagnosed with IBS," said Emily, who just shared her story with you. "That pain I said I was having before my period, when I was eleven—a gastroenterologist told me it was caused by IBS. He told me to try to regulate my bowel movements, and he sent me home. Nobody actually told me after his diagnosis that I didn't have IBS, but I know now that I didn't. It was the endo."

The key question that these doctors commonly fail to ask you, which they should always ask you, is: "Do your symptoms occur at the same time as your period?" Obviously, in Emily's case, she couldn't have answered that because she hadn't had her period yet. But for those who have, the question is vital. If doctors were to ask it, they could consider endo as a diagnosis. Instead, many of them default to IBS. They have you make some adjustments to your diet or prescribe you medication to temporarily calm your bowel symptoms, while giving you the impression that you will heal. Meanwhile, the endo will continue to grow inside you, and the symptoms will return.

Appendicitis, an inflammation of the appendix that can be removed in outpatient surgery (assuming it hasn't burst), is another typical misdiagnosis. The symptoms are similar to endo and IBS: cramps, gassiness, diarrhea, painful urination, and nausea. The general surgeons who perform appendectomies are usually staring straight at the endometriosis when they are removing the appendix, but they either don't recognize or worry about the lesions. So the appendix is removed and the patient recovers relatively quickly, but then the pain starts right up again because the endo is still there. That happened to Meg when she was eighteen.

"Starting when I was ten years old, I was in so much pain that I went to a whole bunch of doctors—a gynecologist, a gastroenterologist, a rheumatologist, a neurologist—and none of them could figure it out," Meg said. "In my senior year of high school I went to the ER, and they said it was probably my appendix. In surgery, they figured out it wasn't my appendix, but they took it out anyway. I went home with one less organ and in the same pain."

If you have pain on the lower right side of your gut, you may very well have appendicitis, but if you have other symptoms of endo, be certain that your doctor knows what endo is and that it can be disqualified as the source of your pain. Losing your appendix is okay—the organ serves no purpose that we know of—but allowing the endo to stay and grow inside you is not okay.

A third common misdiagnosis is with regard to ovarian cysts. These cysts are not unusual; they are a result of the ovulation process each month. They are found on the inside of the ovaries and filled with fluid, which is typically clear. When the fluid is clear, the cysts will usually disappear on their own without any medication.

However, sometimes these cysts can be chocolate cysts, the ones I mentioned that I found in Ileana that can cause extreme pain and other complications. These cysts are the root cause of most advanced endometriosis cases. They eventually rupture or leak and stick to the intestines and pelvic walls. If a doctor tells you that you have ovarian cysts and nothing to worry about, your first question should be, "Are they chocolate cysts?" If they are, then you absolutely have something to worry about—those cysts need to be surgically removed. If the doctor doesn't know, then you need to find a doctor who does, and immediately, before those cysts burst. Having ovarian cysts is one of the most glaring examples of how your knowledge about endo, knowing what questions to ask, and advocating for yourself can make all the difference in your health.

The last frequent "misdiagnosis" I want to discuss is a hysterectomy. I put that word in quotes because a hysterectomy isn't a misdiagnosis. It's a procedure—the removal of the uterus (which could also include the removal of the ovaries, fallopian tubes, and cervix). However, I've included it in this chapter because many doctors perform hysterectomies as a result of a misdiagnosis, which can be emotionally devastating. They will tell you that a hysterectomy is your only solution when it's not.

A hysterectomy is permanent. Once your uterus is removed, it cannot be put back in your body. And when your uterus is gone, so is your ability to have children. Sadly, I've had patients, including teenagers, who had hysterectomies because their previous doctors knew too little about endo, and those doctors incorrectly told them that they had to cut out their wombs. The girls trusted the diagnosis and agreed to do it because they were desperate to make the pain go away. In many cases, the pain persisted after this procedure. If you have endo, removing the uterus will obviously remove any endo that is attached to that organ, but it will not take care of other regions where the endo may have spread. That means the pain will stay, the endo will continue to grow, and you will be back to where you started—but now without your uterus and with no chance of ever giving birth.

Julie, who shared her story in my first book, was fifteen when she was diagnosed with stage IV endo. When she was eighteen, after several unsuccessful surgeries, her doctor at the time recommended that she have a hysterectomy. Given her pain, she reluctantly agreed.

"But six months after the surgery, I started to feel the pain again," Julie said. "It wasn't as bad as before, but it was back." When she finally found me, I was extremely frustrated that a doctor would remove the uterus of an eighteen-year-old. In my opinion, it was unnecessary. The surgery I performed on her was her twelfth surgery. It was also the last one she would need. Unfortunately, though, the damage had been done.

"Part of me is still angry about it, but there is nothing I can do," Julie said. "Now that I'm older and know what I know about the disease, I know how crazy it was for that doctor to do that to me. I just want to prevent it from happening to someone else."

Having a hysterectomy is sometimes necessary, and depending on your age, it may not be a bad thing. But it should be a last resort for treating endo, especially for women who may want to one day have children.

I don't want you to fear that if your doctor diagnoses you with any of the conditions I've discussed, they are probably wrong. They may be absolutely correct and 100 percent qualified to say so. IBS is common. Appendectomies are common. Ovarian cysts often are not chocolate cysts. Hysterectomies can be necessary. But if your doctor gives you one of those diagnoses and cannot rule out endo, you need to find a doctor who can. This is your body, your life. You should never have healthy organs removed or useless medications prescribed.

Think about it this way: would you let a doctor put a cast on your foot without knowing if it might be a sprain? Would you let a doctor administer chemotherapy for cancer if they couldn't be certain that cancer is what you have? Would you let a doctor prescribe you blood pressure medicine without taking your blood pressure? Of course not. I'll say it again: one in every ten women in the United States has endo, yet many people, including doctors, do not know what it is. This is why it's imperative that you know all that you can about the disease. Many of those around you will not be able to comprehend the level of torment you are in. You must make them understand.

My Name Is Stephanie

"I cried in the car all the way home. I felt so defeated."

If there were a contest to determine who was misdiagnosed the most times before being properly diagnosed with endo, I don't know if I'd "win," but I'd probably rank in the upper echelon. An added twist to my journey, as you'll read at the end of my story, is that it would all come full circle.

My stomach pains began in middle school when I was about twelve, and they got progressively worse in high school. I went to my primary care doctor, who referred me to a pediatric gastroenterologist, who confidently diagnosed me with IBS. And that was it. No advice. No meds. The pain was simply going to be my normal.

When I was a senior in high school, a few weeks before graduation, canker sores suddenly developed in my mouth and down my throat. The pain they caused wouldn't allow me to eat. I was sent to a dentist, who sent me to an oral surgeon, who sent me to the hospital. After some tests, they told me I had an intolerance to gluten. This meant I would have to give up, among other delicious foods, my favorite Long Island bagels and pizza. But if that would solve my problems, I was more than happy to do so. Unfortunately, it didn't.

I started college in the fall, and though the canker sores weren't much of an issue anymore, the stomach pain still was, along with a new symptom: constipation. It felt like nothing I ate was being digested. I went to another gastroenterologist, who did a colonoscopy and tested me for fructose and lactose intolerance. The lactose came back positive. So now I was on a no-gluten and no-dairy diet, and I was taking medicine for my constipation.

And the pain continued.

I went to a third gastroenterologist, who ran the same tests as the previous doctor and got the same results. She had me meet with her nutritionist, but again, nothing was solved.

My senior year of college I got a sharp pain on the right side of my abdomen. My mom and I assumed it was my appendix. We went to the hospital for tests, but they came back inconclusive. The hospital sent me to a gynecologist who said, "Maybe you have cysts," but she didn't know for sure. I was also having bladder issues around this time, so I went to another doctor for that. She was the first to bring up the possibility of endo.

"But I doubt that's what you have," she said. Since I had never heard of endo, and since I assumed she would know best, I said okay and moved on. Though her doubt was wrong, I would later be grateful that she at least mentioned the possibility. The seed had been planted in my brain.

In the days after leaving her office, I had another new symptom: bloating. It looked like a balloon was inflating in my stomach. I couldn't put on my jeans, and the pain in my stomach was fierce. With nothing to lose, I did research on that new word *endometriosis* that I'd learned and I came across the term "endo belly"—severe bloating that comes with endo. I had no doubt that's what I had. That's when Mom took me to see her gynecologist for the first time. Since she had gone to him for so long and trusted him, she figured he would know.

"I've never heard of endo belly," he said, "and I'm certain you don't have endometriosis."

Huh?

He suggested that I go on a high dosage of birth control pills. Not only did the pills not calm any of my symptoms, my face broke out unlike ever before, and I wasn't getting my period at all. I tried the pills for four months and hated them.

After I graduated from college the bloating continued. I would get home from work, take off my pants so I could breathe, and lay motionless until work the next morning. I was bloated probably ninety percent of the time every day. I cried a lot, as it had been more than ten years and nothing had changed. I decided that if this had any chance of being solved, I would have to take matters into my own hands and really push the possibility that I had endo.

So, I went to see my primary care doctor, where this all began, and I told him that I thought I had endo. He listened to what I had to say, and instead of pushing endo off the table, he sent me to an endocrinologist who he thought might be able to determine what was causing my symptoms.

"What brings you here?" the endocrinologist asked.

I explained the past decade—the symptoms, the misdiagnoses, the useless treatments, and my own findings on endo. He was very nice, listened unlike any other doctor had, and seemed to be taking copious notes. He then thought about it for a moment and gave me his conclusion.

"I think you should see a specialist for IBS," he said.

And there was the full circle. I was back to where I had started in middle school. From IBS diagnosis to IBS diagnosis, I'd seen a total of thirteen doctors, none of whom could determine what was wrong with my body. I cried in the car all the way home. I felt so defeated.

When I got home, completely desperate and certain that I had endo, I went to Google, where I found Dr. Seckin. His first appointment would have normally been weeks or maybe months out, but he happened to have a cancelation the next day. I felt that was a sign that I'd found the right doctor. When I got to his waiting room, that feeling was confirmed when other patients and I started a conversation about our symptoms. We instantly shared a bond over something that I had no idea others could relate to. For the first time, I felt like I wasn't alone.

To any middle- or high school girls who are in the position today that I was as a twelve-year-old when I was first misdiagnosed with IBS: it is likely that many doctors you'll see will tell you that you can't possibly have endo, because the truth is that most of them have no idea what it is. Maybe if you know that going in, you won't have to go through what I and countless others have gone through. Yes, it's possible that you could have IBS or appendicitis or something else, and there is nothing wrong with being checked for any of that, but you also need to be checked for endo by someone who is qualified to do so. I had doctors who wiped endo right off the table, even though I'd suggested it, because they didn't know any better. But I didn't give up, and you can't either.

CHAPTER 5

Managing Endo Symptoms in Public

Let's forget for a moment what may be causing your symptoms, be it endo or something else, and focus solely on the symptoms themselves: pain, heavy bleeding, bloating, exhaustion, or any of the multitude of other possibilities. Until you can find an answer, you still have to go out in public to some extent—for school, work, social events, or to run errands. You will have to be around people who don't know your condition, and whom you don't want to know about it.

So, how do you manage your day-to-day affairs until you are able to get these symptoms under control? Are there places you should try to avoid going to or things you shouldn't do? What hygiene supplies and other items should you have on hand to get you through a day? You could make up your mind that you're going to do whatever you want, whenever you want, and wherever you want, but the reality is that this disease will make such a goal extremely difficult.

For that reason, it may be a good idea to pause for a moment to ask yourself, *Should I attend this event? Is it worth the hassle? What can I do to go and still be comfortable? Is there a better or easier way to do what I need or want to do?* I think with some planning and precautionary measures, along with some experimentation to figure out best practices, you will find that you can pretty much do whatever you'd like.

You don't want to let these symptoms dictate your life. However, you also don't want to put yourself in precarious situations.

I'm going to let my patient, Winnie, tell you what she has done in the past and what she does today regarding her symptoms. Winnie has had one of the most complicated cases of endometriosis that I've ever dealt with. She is now thirty-two years old and has been battling this disease since she was a teenager. Endo critically damaged her kidney, her bowels, and her uterus. She lost a lot of weight, had several infections, developed sepsis, and needed multiple blood transfusions. The endo in her grew so quickly after the first surgery, which lasted nine hours, I had to do a second one four months later that lasted thirteen hours. It was one of the longest my team and I have ever done.

Winnie still struggles with this disease, though she does feel healthier today and is gradually learning how to live in a way that she hasn't known in nearly two decades. Some symptoms persist given the magnitude of her disease. Hence, she is prepared wherever she goes. Her suggestions may not all be the right ones for you, but they will give you some ideas of how to plan ahead, or they may spark some new ideas that would better fit your circumstances.

My Name Is Winnie

"Be prepared."

One thing I want to note about my condition that Dr. Seckin did not mention is that when my endometriosis was at its worst, I had six days a month during my period that were absolutely horrifying in terms of pain and bleeding. The other twenty-five days or so my symptoms were manageable enough that I could go out and be active. Six days out of thirty-one may not sound like many, but when you're a student, that's the equivalent of about two months over the course of the school year. Or, when those six days happen to be during a holiday, family vacation, or milestone event, they are long and depressing days. Though I'm doing much better today, I still have symptoms and am careful about what activities I do around the time of my period. The key phrase that I want you to take from everything that I am about to share is "Be prepared." You don't ever want to be caught not having what you need nearby. If it can't be on your person, you need to have a short and direct line to it at all times and be able to access it quickly. Endo is not going to hold off its attack while you finish what you are doing or while you go from one place to another. Immediately having what you need will help you avoid embarrassment, have the fewest disruptions, and have the confidence to continue doing what you want to do.

Let's start with the obvious: every girl with endometriosis who has symptoms of painful periods and heavy bleeding needs to carry plenty of tampons and pads. A change or two (or three) of clothes is also a good idea. Quantities will depend on how long you will be gone, but make sure you have more than enough to last the entire time. Don't say to yourself, "There's a store near where we're going; I'll pick up more there if I need to." When endo strikes, you need to be ready, not ready to go do what you need to do to be ready. Take the time in advance to properly prepare. It will relieve a lot of mental stress.

When it comes to traveling long distances or going away for extended periods of time when I know it will be during my period, I generally follow one rule: I don't go. Yes, that sounds discouraging, and it can be, especially if we're talking about family vacations or holiday travel, but you have to weigh the pros and cons. My parents are from China, and many times when they've traveled there to see my grandparents, I haven't gone. Being on a plane for sixteen hours with endo symptoms is not appealing. Staying in the comfort of my own home to take care of myself is.

With that said, I have broken my own rule at times. When I was in college, I did a three-month study abroad program in Italy. It was a risk, but I really wanted to do it. For the trip, I brought several essentials, including a heating pad, the correct electrical adapters for the heating pad (Europe's electrical outlets are different from ours in the United States), and my own food.

I packed enough instant oatmeal bags to have breakfast every morning of my stay. My mom bought me various nuts that are good for digestion—pistachios, walnuts, and cashews—and grinded them up and put them in baggies for me to sprinkle on other food. I stayed away from all dairy, which could trigger inflammation, and I brought a lot of vitamins to keep up my energy. I also packed some anti-inflammatory herbal supplements, such as turmeric, and I left behind all narcotics. You will learn, if you haven't already, what foods are good specifically for your body. Pack plenty of them. Even if you are traveling domestically by car, don't be caught hungry with nothing to eat. You don't want to be forced to eat whatever is nearby, such as fast food or food from a vending machine at a rest stop. Don't use your time away as an excuse to "cheat" on what you eat; the endo could make you pay for it in some frightening ways.

When I was in high school, I kept two water bottles in my locker, along with a gallon of Pedialyte. Pedialyte, which is associated with infants and kids, can also be for adults. It contains electrolytes that will elevate hydration. I kept it at school because there were days during my period when I didn't want to eat, but I needed fluids to get me through the day until I could get home and crash in my bed. I also kept a blood pressure monitor and thermometer in my locker to know what I needed to do if an attack occurred. While a school nurse may have those items, it's nice to have them at your disposal. Something else I had available to me daily was ibuprofen for the pain and some vitamins for energy. All of that may need to be approved by your school for you to possess and consume, but administrators should be fine with it if they know the purpose.

Speaking of needing approval, I often had to suddenly use the bathroom when I was in class, which required a hall pass. To avoid being questioned in front of the other students, I explained my condition in advance to each of my teachers and provided them with some information from endofound.org so that when I asked to go, they would quietly and swiftly oblige. Some of them allowed a friend to go with me to be sure I was okay. You may need to educate your teachers about it, but once they understand, you shouldn't have any pushback. If you do, go to your principal or have your parents explain it. You shouldn't need your doctor to get involved, but have him or her jump in if necessary. Do whatever you need to do to be as comfortable as possible. You shouldn't have to go through red tape at school every time your endo flares up.

Something else that I use today that would be beneficial in school, at work, or anywhere away from home is an app called

"Calm." It has meditation and calming techniques that will work on the spot. For example, if you are anxiously laying on the floor in pain in a public bathroom stall, you can access Calm, which will give you instant breathing techniques and help settle your nerves. It's like having a friend there with you coaching you on how to breathe and relax. It won't rid you of your pain or bleeding, but it can help you retain some mental focus until you can get help from someone or move to a place where you can better take care of yourself.

Another item that I have, and I think it's one of the most important things that anyone with endo can have, is an ER bag. It's a simple duffel bag that I have packed at all times and sitting by the door, ready to grab as I head out to the emergency room. That may sound overkill to someone without this disease, but most of us with endo have spent many days and nights in emergency rooms. The purpose of the bag is to have everything you would need in the hospital if you are admitted. The hospital may have some of these items, but if you've been to a hospital overnight, you know how overworked nurses are and how long it could take to get what you need.

My ER bag consists of a heating pad, vitamins, a bottle of Pedialyte, a toothbrush, toothpaste, pads, a T-shirt, pajama pants, and three pairs of underwear. If you're bleeding heavily, you'll be happy to have your own underwear instead of having to use the paper underwear a hospital might give you.

Another must for the bag, if you have long hair, is hair ties. Nearly all women with endo throw up, and you don't want to have to wash your hair in a hospital. It's too much work, plus they don't have hair dryers.

I'd also pack a charger for your phone, noise-canceling headphones (if you own a pair) to help you sleep, a towel, and a comfortable pillow. Hospitals will obviously have a blood pressure reader and thermometer, like I kept in my locker, but I'd still pack them if you have them. Sometimes I like to monitor myself if a nurse hasn't been by in a while.

Finally, pack your own food in the bag. Have you ever had hospital food? It's not the best. Or, have you tried to get hospital food when you've checked in at midnight? It's not going to happen. Again, pack snacks that are good for your body and have a long shelf life, like nuts. You don't want to be scrounging through your kitchen cupboards when you should be on your way to the hospital. The ER bag should be packed and ready so that you have nothing to think about other than to grab it and go.

If everything I've discussed sounds overwhelming, it can be—at least until you get used to it. But imagine how much worse things will be if you're not prepared or don't take precautions before you travel, go to school, go to work, or rush to the ER.

One final note on being prepared: don't be afraid to plan a year or more in advance around your period. When I was in college picking my classes in August, I calculated when my period would occur the following May and matched it to the dates of when the finals would be in each class. If I found that a final was going to fall during my period, I wouldn't take that class. As extreme as that may sound, it wasn't at all come May. I knew I'd be able to study for my tests in all my classes and take all the tests without any glaring distractions from the endo. You can do the same for vacations or spending weekends with friends or going to concerts. The more time you put into preparing for the effects of this disease, the more you will be able to manage it and accomplish what you want to accomplish.

I may not travel as much as I'd like or go out with friends all the time. I may spend more time in the ER than I'd like. I may not be able to do something spontaneous if it falls during those six days each month. But I'm genuinely a happier person because I've learned to get ahead of this disease. I know that the further ahead of it I can get with my preparedness, the more I will be able to live with joy and comfort.

II

I Think I May Have Endo. Now What?

Every girl with endometriosis needs help defeating the disease. Not just help from medical professionals but from parents, guardians, sisters, brothers, friends, teachers, coaches—people who spend quality time with you every day. I know reaching out can be easier said than done. Endo has the sinister ability to make those closest to you doubt you, which in turn can cause you to doubt yourself. This is why it is vital that you trust what you feel and do everything possible to be heard and believed.

CHAPTER 6

Who Can I Ask for Help? And When?

It is my hope that you have a close and loving relationship with your mother. To be able to approach the woman who gave birth to you to discuss something as intimate and sensitive as your period and the pain associated with it is invaluable. She is the first person I'd recommend you speak to about it if you can. However, I know that's not necessarily the case for everyone. Some girls don't know their mothers and are raised by their fathers or grandparents or other family members. Some have lost their mothers to death. Some have strong bonds with their mothers, but conversations about their periods are too awkward to have or taboo in their cultures. Some mothers will tell their daughters to "get through it like I did." That attitude isn't from a lack of love, but a lack of understanding.

So, if your mother is not an option, then to whom do you turn?

Every girl's situation will be different, but I can try to navigate you through it in a broad sense to find that right person. Just be assured that there *is* someone out there whom you can count on.

Think about all of the people you trust who could possibly guide you through this adversity. It could be, in no particular order, your grandmother, an older sister, a close friend, a close friend's mother, an aunt, or someone in authority at school, such as a teacher or a coach, or your doctor. The right person to support you might even be a trusted male figure.

It may seem strange to consider talking to a grandmother about this. Grandmothers naturally seem old to us when we're young, but your grandmother likely isn't as old as you think. Depending on when she had her children and when your parents had you, your grandmother may not have entered menopause that long ago. Even if it has been a while, as a woman she can have an intelligent conversation with you about your period. It's also possible that she had painful periods or endo herself. If your grandmother is a prominent figure in your life, take advantage of your relationship with her by trying to talk to her about it. You may be surprised how much she's been through and how much she can help.

Sisters and close friends can also be good sources of assistance. Understand that if they aren't much older than you or if they recently got their first period, they may not be comfortable discussing this with you because they don't have a lot of knowledge themselves. They also may not understand your pain because their periods may be perfectly normal, and they may think that every girl feels the same way with her periods. But if your friendship is a close one, you might be able to convince them that what is happening to you is beyond the norm, enough that they will be sympathetic and try to help.

You may have a teacher at school with whom you have a special bond. Maybe you could ask her if you could talk after school or during her free period about a personal issue. Teachers are instinctively nurturing and wouldn't be in the line of work they are in if they weren't.

Like teachers, nurturing is in the blood of nurses. You should be able to count on them to get you what you need. They can also refer you to a gynecologist, as can your pediatrician, which I will discuss in a moment.

School counselors may also be able to assist. They are trained to help students overcome any barriers that could hinder their learning, such as hunger, illness, or a learning disability. If you're not in school or not doing well in class, counselors care. I can't tell you that they will be specifically trained on menstrual periods, but if your pain prevents you from functioning or if you are absent as a result, they will have or know where to find the resources you need.

Could you go to your dad or another male friend in the family? Absolutely. Clearly, no man is going to be able to directly relate to what you are feeling. Many won't know how your period works or all of the personal hygiene products you need. But they will do what they can because they won't want to see you suffer. They will find some way to take care of you, even if it means finding a woman in their lives whom they trust to step in.

And, of course, there is your pediatrician, the doctor you hopefully see at least once a year for a checkup and to get your vaccinations. As I've said, not all pediatricians are going to know a lot about endo, but if you explain to yours how you feel, they should help you. That help may come in the way of a referral to a gynecologist or an OB/GYN (obstetrician/gynecologist), and either would be fine. A gynecologist is a specialist in women's reproductive health; an OB/GYN also cares for women during and after pregnancy. The American College of Obstetricians and Gynecologists recommends girls first see a gynecologist between the ages of thirteen and fifteen, but sooner is certainly fine if you're feeling endo symptoms. If the gynecologist you are referred to makes you uncomfortable, isn't listening to you, or doesn't appear to be helping, ask your pediatrician to refer you to a different one. You could also ask family members or friends whom they go to, or you could search for a reputable one online.

One way to bolster your chances of being understood by and getting help from any of the people I've mentioned, especially your doctor, is to gather evidence to back up your claims. And one of the best ways to do that is to keep a diary, one that tracks data. It can be a simple spreadsheet. Presenting a doctor or anyone else with detailed evidence of what you've been through each day for a few months or more can only strengthen your case.

Without a diary, you are trusting everybody to take your word on what you say you are and have been feeling, and while they may want to believe you, they may have doubts because they cannot comprehend what you are experiencing. They likely have never heard of anyone having such pain from her period and may assume you are being dramatic, so they may not take your claims as seriously as they should.

And if they don't listen to you about your pain, you may do what most girls with endo do: stop complaining and quietly suffer. As a result, your grades could drop, and your ability to perform effectively in athletic, dance, or academic competitions could falter. Your job performance could slip, causing your coworkers or customers to get upset. You could be isolated from everything and everyone you know and love—all because you don't know what's happening to your body, and because nobody is willing to listen to you or believe you when you describe how awful it is.

At my foundation's website, www.endofound.org, we have a "Personal Pain Profile: Daily Symptom Tracker" that is designed specifically for anyone who has endo symptoms to show to their physician. The chart has a square for each day of the month. In each square you enter the date and note any symptoms you may be feeling, such as pain, bloating, heavy bleeding, exhaustion, or digestive issues. There is also a page with a picture of the front and back of the human body. Use that to mark where you are feeling pain and if it is during your period, at any other time of the month, or both. Showing this chart to your doctor should assist them when trying to determine if you might have endo or some other disease or condition. If they won't consider what you've recorded, find a doctor who will listen.

I recommend that you document your findings for three to six months; the more information you can collect, the easier it should be to state your case and for a diagnosis to be reached. If you just had your first period and you hand your doctor a chart a couple of weeks later that shows a few days of pain, that probably won't help much. With that said, if you are totally miserable after a short time with no signs of improvement, take whatever findings you have immediately to your doctor to see what he or she says. Don't try to hold out if you can't.

Just because you're trying to keep track of how bad you feel doesn't mean you should stop doing what you can to get well during this time, though. If taking a couple of Advil makes you feel better, then do it. Just be sure to note on your chart when you took it and how long it provided relief. If changing the foods you eat or exercising makes you feel better, note the new foods you're eating or the exercises you're doing. Understanding what you're doing to try to manage your pain should not make your doctor less likely to take your chart seriously. The more information you can provide your doctor, the better.

Something else you can do to boost your case while you're tracking data is gather evidence from others. For example, you could have a teacher explain in a letter what she has seen you endure during class. Or, on those days that you were home from school, what anecdotal evidence can your mother or another family member provide to show that you were truly ill? And they shouldn't just say that they witnessed you in a lot of pain; they should be descriptive, like, "She was in so much pain that she was sprawled on the bathroom floor all afternoon and could only get up long enough to vomit in the toilet." They may not understand what's happening to you, but they can still describe what they see.

Two final notes:

First, while endo can and will grow if left untreated, in most cases it will not spread so quickly that you won't have time to track the symptoms. In other words, if I do surgery on you today, the endo I find probably won't be too far advanced from what I would have found had I done the surgery a few weeks or a few months ago. There are exceptions, such as the case Ileana described in the first section, but they are rare. If you can tolerate the symptoms, know that the more hard data and anecdotal evidence you can gather, along with any knowledge you can gain about the disease, the easier it will be for you to confidently speak up and present a solid case.

Second, regarding the people who can help you while you are gathering this evidence, the examples I gave are some of the most obvious ones. If you're close to an athletic coach, a person with whom one of your parents works, a neighbor, or one of your mom's friends, don't be afraid to speak up to them. No matter how desperate you may feel or how fruitless your effort may seem, someone will listen. The harder you look and the more you talk about your circumstances, the better chance you will have of finding that right person soon.

My Name Is Melissa

*"I know there are girls who need help
but have nobody to turn to;
I was one of those girls."*

My quest to find someone willing to help me in my fight against endo didn't start well, but I refused to quit. After bouncing around for years from my grandma to the school nurse to multiple doctors and surgeons, I finally found help from an unknown person on a message board, and eventually at Dr. Seckin's "Patient Awareness Day," which is open each year to the public. I don't think that I'll ever be completely well because of how aggressive the endo is, but I'm doing as well as can be expected. Now I'm one of the leading endo advocates in Michigan, trying to provide young girls with the guidance that I struggled to find.

I started having painful periods when I was about fourteen. Any day of school I missed I spent rocking back and forth on my couch in tears. I don't know if my mom had endo—my paternal grandma raised me. When I tried to talk to my grandma about it back then, she said, "Oh, yeah, I had the same thing. It's normal."

I fought through the "normal" the best I could, but some days the pain was too much to bear. One afternoon I went to the school nurse when the pain caused me to break into a sweat.

"Melissa," she said with considerable concern, "are you on drugs?"

I went to her for help for my pain, and she accused me of being a drug addict. This is what high school was like most days and every month during my period. I couldn't even attend my own graduation ceremony because I had my period that day.

With the idea that this was normal ingrained in my mind, and without a doctor or anyone else able to offer me any relief, I suffered for the next decade. When I was twenty-four I was sick in some way every day. You name it, I had it: nausea, killer cramps, headaches, fatigue, painful bowels. I was reduced to eating nothing but crackers and broth. I finally went to a gastroenterologist who diagnosed me with IBS. When I got home I googled my symptoms and compared them to IBS symptoms. I knew immediately that I didn't have IBS. I then found an article that said sixty to eighty percent of women diagnosed with IBS actually have something called endometriosis. So, I went to the bookstore, found a book on endo, and laid on the floor in tears reading all about it. There was no doubt that endo was what I had.

One reason I was so sure was because every day for nearly a year I had been keeping a diary of my symptoms and how they made me feel. I found trends that I hadn't noticed during years prior because I hadn't been recording anything. For example, I was nauseated a lot, but I couldn't quantify it until I started keeping track. During that year, I learned that I was nauseated 80 percent of the time.

Armed with data that helped me validate my claims, I went to my OB/GYN and gave her my self-diagnosis. She listened to me and read my notes, did an ultrasound, found a large cyst on my ovary, and performed laser surgery.

"I've never seen anything that bad in my life," she said when I awoke. "There was endo everywhere. I did the best I could."

She didn't give me any context as to what any of that meant. She just prescribed me birth control pills and wished me luck. But what I had needed was far more than a pill and good wishes. Six months after the surgery I could hardly function at work or go out with friends, but I forced myself through it as I thought this was normal. The pain and nausea crippled me. It was devastating.

I went online again and found an endo chatroom where a woman talked about laparoscopic deep-excision surgery. I'd never heard of it, and I wasn't about to let her go until I learned all about it. I hit her hard with questions. What were her symptoms? How was this surgery different from laser? How was she feeling now? She was happy to reply to every question I had. She was the first person who really understood me, who could relate to me, who knew the pain. All these years, and it took a stranger to come through. She referred me to her surgeon in Georgia, so off I went.

The surgery itself went well—I was in stage IV, and he cleaned out a lot of endo—but I had an allergic reaction to a sealant he used afterward that was supposed to prevent scar tissue from forming. I had to take steroids for two months. They worked, but a year later the pain had returned. I went back to Georgia where the same surgeon removed more endo and some scar tissue that had grown since the last surgery; this is how aggressive it was. I was good again, but only for another year. In more pain but unable to afford another trip to Georgia, I went to an imaging center near my home in Michigan for an ultrasound, at which time a large cyst was detected. I found a local doctor who said he could do surgery, but almost immediately after opening me up, he was finished.

"I couldn't do anything," he said when I awoke.

Seriously, he wasn't kidding. He opened me, took one glance inside, and closed me. I was in the operating room for like twenty minutes. Imagine what the endo must have looked like to scare a surgeon like that. I was fortunate enough soon after to be able to find another surgeon who wasn't so intimidated and who removed a grapefruit-sized cyst and one of my ovaries. That was my fifth surgery.

Overall, I was feeling much better than I had been prior to my first excision surgery in Georgia, when all of these surgeries began. I was still in some pain, and I'd accepted that more surgeries would be necessary because of how fast the endo was growing, but I was at least able to take some Advil and function day to day. That's how my life would remain for about the next ten years.

In my late thirties, I read about Dr. Seckin's "Patient Awareness Day" he holds each spring in New York City. I'd become a vocal advocate in Michigan, talking to people through social media and on the radio about endo, and I'd also opened my own protein bar business. I went to Dr. Seckin's conference to meet him to see what more I could learn about the disease. After introducing myself and telling him my story, he asked me how I'd been feeling.

"Not so great lately," I said.

Before I knew it, I'd set up an appointment with him and had surgery. He removed all the endo he could find, along with part of my bowel, which was wrapped in endo. It took me about five months to recover, and I feel the best that I've felt since my pre-pubescent days. I'm not one hundred percent—I may never be—but I've come to terms with that.

After my surgery, while talking about it with my aunt, she gave me some startling information: my grandma who raised me (my aunt's mother) had a hysterectomy when she was in her thirties and likely had endo. Unfortunately, my grandma was old and in a nursing home when I was told this, so I never could have that conversation with her. Why didn't Grandma tell me about her hysterectomy when I was teenager complaining about how painful my period was? Why did she tell me that what I felt was normal? Probably because her generation didn't talk about stuff like that, and I bet she really believed it was normal. I'd also wager no doctor ever uttered the word "endometriosis" to her. They probably told her she needed a hysterectomy, she said okay, they removed her uterus, and she felt better. I don't blame her for not sharing that with me, but imagine how much sooner I may have been able to be diagnosed and treated if she and I could have had that conversation when I was fourteen.

My niece is fifteen now and having painful cramps, and I'm watching her like a hawk. I feel that it's my responsibility to fill her head with the knowledge she needs to protect her body, and I will do it for anyone, whether I know them or not. I feel this is my duty after years of suffering. I do not want anyone to suffer as long as I have. I know there are girls who have nobody to turn to; I was one of those girls. I now talk to strangers daily to tell them my story in hopes of comforting them so they know they're not alone and providing them guidance to help them get the right treatment sooner. If I hadn't found that woman in the chatroom, who knows where I'd be today. Don't ever stop looking for that someone you can turn to. They are out there somewhere; trust me. As in my case, it may even be someone you don't know yet.

CHAPTER 7

Help Yourself by Knowing Your Family History

One of the first questions a doctor will (or should) ask someone with chronic symptoms of any kind is, "Does this run in your family?" Your knowledge of your family's health history could help a doctor diagnose you or suggest preventive measures for conditions or diseases to which you may be susceptible.

According to the U.S. National Library of Medicine:

> "Families have many factors in common, including their genes, environment, and lifestyle. Together, these factors can give clues to medical conditions that may run in a family. By noticing patterns of disorders among relatives, healthcare professionals can determine whether an individual, other family members, or future generations may be at an increased risk of developing a particular condition."

If nobody in your family before you had a certain disease or condition, that doesn't mean you are immune to it. Conversely, if your family has a long history of contracting a certain disease or condition, you won't necessarily get it. But the more presence it has in a family's genetic link, the more prone to it you are. Some examples include diabetes, heart disease, high cholesterol, high blood pressure, cancer, depression, Alzheimer's, bipolar disorder— and endometriosis.

As I've stated, if your mom or sister has or had endo, you are six times more likely to get it. And if you do, your daughters are at even greater risk.

It's shocking that endo, documented as far back as four thousand years, can remain in the relative state of anonymity it's in if it is genetically linked. But how can it gain any awareness when people don't talk about it, even within their own families, because of the taboos associated with it or because it's continually misdiagnosed? Famous nineteenth- and twentieth-century neurologist Sigmund Freud diagnosed many women with hysteria, though it's now believed that what those women really had was endo. Others during Freud's time would diagnose symptoms women had as being the result of witchcraft or demons. Again, many believe today that these diagnoses should have actually been endo.

Can you imagine walking into a doctor's office with that much pain during your period every month and being told that demons must be the culprit? I would argue that what many girls with endo encounter today in doctors' offices isn't far off from that. Whether you're told that the pain you are feeling is in your head, that it's normal, or that it's the work of demons, the result is the same: the doctor is dismissing what you are saying and sending you home without any viable solutions, leaving you frustrated, lost, and still in pain.

So, since generations of girls dating back thousands of years were silenced when they sought help, and since the disease remains relatively unknown today, it should come as no surprise to you that your mother or grandmother or other women in your family could have had endo and never told you. In fact, it's possible that *they* didn't know they had it because they weren't properly diagnosed. To this day, they may think that what they went through was normal, so they won't mention it to you or act with urgency when you have the same pain. You just read that scenario in Melissa's story involving her grandma. Here's another one.

Casey experienced a high level of pain in middle school and high school. Her periods were heavy, and she missed a lot of school and wasn't able to play sports.

"But I didn't think it was unusual because a lot of women in my family had had bad periods," Casey said. "My mom had them for years, and I witnessed it. I always saw her in pain, but when I questioned her, she would say, 'That's what happens when you have five kids.' She'd never heard of endo. No doctor had ever mentioned it to her."

Casey saw gastroenterologists and other doctors who ran many of tests, but they came up with nothing. When a gynecologist finally referred her to me, after four or five years, I did surgery and found endo. That's when her mother realized that her own pain may have had nothing to do with having five children.

"She figured maybe she should get checked out, and a month after I did she had her own surgery and found out she had endo," Casey said. "She was finished having kids, so she had her uterus removed, and now she's pain-free. I know it's unusual for a mom to discover endo and have surgery for it after her daughter, but that's what happened. When she realized I had it and that it could be genetic, she knew she probably had it too. I do have a fear, if I have daughters one day, that they will get it, but at least now we know what it is and that the possibility is definitely there."

These stories are why it is so vital for families to share their medical histories with those who share their genes.

How do you find out your family history? Since medical records are private to each individual, about the only way to do it is to ask members of your family. The U.S. National Library of Medicine says:

"The easiest way to get information about family medical history is to talk to relatives about their health. Have they had any medical problems, and when did they occur? A family gathering could be a good time to discuss these issues. Additionally, obtaining medical records and other documents (such as obituaries and death certificates) can help complete a family medical history. It is important to keep this information up-to-date and to share it with a healthcare professional regularly."

I would suggest going straight to your mother, grandmother, aunts, and cousins, and asking them about their histories. These may not be easy conversations, and they may have to be done individually rather than in a group for each person to be comfortable. If you ask and tell them why you are asking, including explaining your own pain, I would hope they would share with you the information you are seeking. They may still say, "I was told it was normal, so you, too, are going to have to fight through it." But you can counter with some education: "That may have been the case in your day, but now we know about this disease called endometriosis, and I think I may have it."

Some of you may not be able to get your family history easily, if at all. Maybe you were adopted and have no medical records from your biological family. That was the case for Stephanie, the one who had seen thirteen doctors and was diagnosed twice with IBS.

"My brother and I were both adopted and don't know our birth parents," Stephanie said. "So anytime I went to the doctor and was asked about my medical history, I'd have to tell them that I didn't know and couldn't find out. It definitely made the process tougher because the doctors had nothing to go off of."

Records can also be difficult to obtain due to the deaths of relatives, or maybe because living relatives won't talk. Medical procedures, especially if they involve the reproductive anatomy, are so personal to some people that they won't talk about them under any circumstances, even with their own flesh and blood. That's how it was for Dilara who told you that her mother is from Turkey, where women's health issues are rarely discussed.

"I found out that right around the time I had my surgery, my aunt had been diagnosed with endometriosis; I knew nothing about it," Dilara said. "She ended up having surgery and somehow was able to keep it quiet. I asked my mom why she didn't tell me about my aunt given my situation, but she said even she didn't know about it. That's how silent it was kept."

Even if you can't get the information you are seeking from your family, it's no excuse for a doctor to not be able to properly diagnose you. But it's definitely worth the effort to try to get whatever records you can.

One final thought: keep meticulous records of your own medical history. Whether it's endo or something else, any diseases or conditions you may have could serve future generations of men and women in your family. You never know—information you keep today that you provide in the future could save the life of your child or grandchild.

My Name Is Ali

"If your uterus or vagina hurts,
society says we aren't supposed to talk about it?"

I got my first period when I was thirteen. I had some pain but nothing terrible. That changed at fifteen when it became debilitating. I missed a lot of school. The advice offered from friends and family was, "Take some Midol." When that didn't work, they said I was being dramatic, that this was womanhood, and I believed them.

At sixteen, I bled for sixty days at a time. Yeah, sixty days. I don't recall a time that I didn't have a tampon. I would go to school, go to work, and come home with blood-stained clothes. Despite what everyone had said, I knew there was nothing normal about this.

I went to a gynecologist who tried four different birth control pills. They decreased the pain, but I didn't like the side effects, so I stopped taking them. When I was seventeen I did my own research online and learned about endo for the first time. I took the information to the same gynecologist, who said, "You're too young to have this." I refused to accept that. I told her to do surgery or I'd find a new gynecologist. So she did. It was laser surgery.

"Yep, you had endo," she said when I woke up. She said I was somewhere between stages II and III, but that I shouldn't have been in as much pain as I claimed to have been.

Um, but I was.

I asked her if she knew how I got endo.

"No," she said. "We really don't know what endo is to begin with. There's no evidence of where it comes from. Some think it's hereditary, but there's no proof of that."

So this gynecologist who does surgery on endo patients first told me that I didn't have endo, did surgery only after I demanded it, confirmed my personal diagnosis, said nobody really knows what endo is, and said it's not hereditary. She also said that I was likely infertile as a result of the endo and would probably not be able to have children. And that was it. No more explanation. No follow-up appointment. I was released supposedly endo-free.

At eighteen I got married, and my husband and I wanted to have children, but two other gynecologists I went to for second and third opinions agreed that having kids was not going to be possible. So, we went to an endo/fertility specialist who gave us some hope.

"You might be able to get pregnant if I immediately start in vitro fertilization," she said. Commonly known as IVF, it would have meant extracting my eggs and combining them with my husband's sperm in a lab to create an embryo, then putting the embryo into my uterus. I said thanks, but no thanks. I wasn't interested in doing that without first trying to get pregnant naturally.

A year later, guess who was pregnant?

Today we have a healthy three-year-old daughter.

Again, everybody was wrong.

After my pregnancy, the endo symptoms returned. I found Dr. Seckin online and had surgery. He told me that my symptoms were caused by more endo he found and scar tissue that had been created by the laser surgery. Today, I'm an advocate for laparoscopic deep-excision surgery and am adamant that no girl have endo removed through laser surgery.

What does all of this have to do with knowing your family's medical history? Well, after I had my laser surgery, I was telling my grandma and my aunt (my grandma's daughter and dad's sister) about it.

"Oh, yeah, we both had that," my aunt said. "It sucks, doesn't it?"

It sucks? Yes, it sucks! And they both had endo? Not only that, they both had hysterectomies when they were in their forties, my grandma about fifty years ago and my aunt twenty years ago. While I had daily pain and heavy bleeding as a young teen, and was told that it was part of womanhood and that I was being dramatic, they were sitting on this information and never thought to say, "Hey, maybe you have what we had"?

No, they didn't. But I don't blame them for that, for a few reasons.

First, neither of their generations talked about their periods or having hysterectomies; it was all too personal. They quietly did what they had to do to get better and didn't discuss it with anyone. Second, they were never officially told by their doctors that they had endo, even though they know today that's what it was. They were simply told that if they had their uteruses removed, their pain would go away. I would bet their doctors, especially my grandma's way back in the day, didn't know what they were staring at when they opened her up and saw the endo; they just knew it was something that didn't belong there. Third, they never thought it was hereditary. Heck, my gynecologist well into the twenty-first century said to me that it wasn't hereditary.

But now, with all that we know about endo, that culture must change.

I have already put my daughter on an anti-inflammatory diet—no gluten, soy, or dairy—in anticipation of her having endo in ten years. I also consciously buy only non-toxic household products, because many of the standard ones that most people use daily contain hormone distributors. In addition, we are going to openly talk about her periods and endo when it's time, and I will see to it that she is not dismissed by anyone if she experiences endo symptoms. She is going to know all about my medical history, as well as that of her great-grandmother and great-aunt. And I am going to teach her the importance of sharing her history and ours with her own children one day.

If your arm aches, people will listen. If your uterus or vagina hurts, society says we aren't supposed to talk about it? Even within our own families? That's unacceptable. It's an attitude that must change worldwide for this disease to be eradicated, and I will do all that I can to make it happen. Do your best to learn as much as possible about your family's medical history, and keep track of your own so your daughters or nieces or other girls with blood ties to you don't have to suffer. The more family members know about each other, the better chance they have of getting ahead of diseases.

CHAPTER 8

Empowerment

With all that you've read thus far—the personal stories, what endo is, what it isn't, and the steps to take to approach treatment—I can assure you that you know more about this disease than most men and women in the world, even more than some doctors. For something that has afflicted so many women and their families for centuries, that's powerful.

Before I discuss various ways to manage this disease, I want you to understand the important key you now hold. You know why you didn't know much, if anything, about endo prior to this book: because it's continuously been diagnosed as something it's not, because it's not required knowledge to becoming a doctor, because the women who have spoken out for millennia about its devastating symptoms have been ignored. But that tide is changing, and we all need to be part of that change.

The women who have shared their stories about battling this disease, in both my first book and in this one, are heroes. I know my words that explain the disease are important, but they don't equate to the firsthand accounts you've read and will continue to read from these women. They were in your shoes as young women, lost and without hope, but because they have so bravely spoken up, they have given *you* hope. They have provided you with proof to convince those around you that you are telling the truth about your pain and that it's not normal.

What I want you to know, as you read ahead about potential treatments, how to handle the social aspects of having this disease,

and more incredible stories from women who have fought this battle, is that you can feel empowered. Because of the knowledge you
now have and the additional knowledge you are about to gain, you
no longer have to be undiagnosed or misdiagnosed or shunned. You
will not agonize for years or decades as many women have. And
girls who come after you, like Ali's three-year-old daughter you just
read about, will no longer feel lost and hopeless.

Miranda, who had a family history of endo, received surgery
by me when she was seventeen, within one year of her symptoms
starting. Knowing how lucky she was to catch it that soon, Miranda
has made it her mission to help others.

"My mom and I read a lot about endo, which has helped me and
has helped a lot of people I know," Miranda said. "I try to share what
I've learned and experienced when I can in appropriate situations
because it's part of who I am, and I generally get a good reaction.
Sometimes people are confused because they haven't heard of endo,
and I have to do a lot of explaining, but they listen and are interested. It gets girls thinking about it. A lot of them have said that they
have the same symptoms, but they didn't know the probable cause
until I explained it. If I'm grateful for anything about this disease, it's
that it has given me a story to share with others."

Eva, who spoke to you about doctors shrugging off her painful
periods as nothing, also spoke up after surgery.

"I was out of school for quite a while because of my surgery
and the recovery time. When I returned, a lot of people asked me
where I'd been," Eva said. "So, I told my whole class what I'd been
through. They were all supportive, though most of them were
shocked because they'd never heard of endo and couldn't believe
what it had done to me. What shocked me was what happened after
my talk, when a lot of girls came up to me and said, 'I have this too.'
I had no idea."

Right now, *your* health is the most important issue. Focus on what you need to do to get well. But once you've been properly treated and are in a comfortable place, don't stop talking about it. Consider Melissa, and take this to social media, radio, and blogs. Consider Miranda, and take this to your girlfriends. Consider Eva, and take this into the classroom. Or consider Bankes, whose story you will read next. She not only talked about the disease at school like Eva but she's also pushing for schools to make changes in their curriculum to include women's reproductive health.

Share what you've gone through with your family, friends, or coworkers. We've built a strong and compassionate support system in the endo community, but we need more women and girls who are willing to speak up and break the stigma. We need you to help us help future generations.

My Name Is Bankes

*"I believe those of us with endo have
a responsibility to try to change the culture."*

My endo story is like that of so many other girls. I got my first period at twelve years old, and it came with a lot of pain that lasted for years. When I went to Italy on vacation with my family, I couldn't tour the Vatican because my endo flared up and I couldn't walk. One year, on Thanksgiving Day, I spent the entire holiday in bed because I couldn't move. Last year, at the start of my senior year of high school, I was attending school just once a week for several weeks and missing all of the milestone senior activities. Finally, about midway through that year, my gynecologist diagnosed me with endo—but she didn't think I needed surgery. My aunt, who had had endo and, as a result, fertility issues much of her life, disagreed. At her and my mom's insistence, I had laparoscopic deep-excision surgery almost immediately, and now I am pain-free.

I don't know what lies ahead for me, but I can assure you that I will never allow this chronic disease to control me again, and I will do everything in my power to make sure it doesn't do to other girls what it did to me for six years.

My message to you is this: be empowered! Be empowered first for yourself, then for the other girls who have this disease today, and for those who will one day get it. If it weren't for my aunt having the courage to tell me and my mom about her endo and the horror it put her through, we would have listened to my gynecologist's advice, and I shudder thinking about where I'd be today. So many people don't know about or talk about this disease because of the ridiculous taboo that exists with a girl's period. I believe those of us with endo have a responsibility to try to change the culture.

The first thing I did when I returned to school after recovering from surgery was ask my biology teacher if I could talk to the class about endo. She obliged, giving me the entire period to discuss it and take questions. I told my class about my circumstances in great detail, including my painful cramps, what the disease did to my uterus, and the surgery. Nearly every one of them had never heard of endo.

One of the few who did know about it was one of my closest friends. She has endo, though I didn't know until she told me after the presentation. She is on medication for it, but it hasn't helped much; she is still in a lot of pain. I've tried to get her to see my surgeon, but with no luck. You see, her family is from Portugal, a country where talking about periods is traditionally more taboo than in America, even among mothers and daughters. So while my mother is sharing my story all over social media to try to bring awareness to endo, my friend's mother will barely talk to her own daughter about it. There isn't much I can do other than continually remind my friend that I'm here for her, which I do frequently. I can't force her or her mother to do something, but I'm not giving up. I do have hope that my advocacy will one day cause her to take me up on my offer so that she can reclaim and enjoy her life.

After my presentation, I went to school administrators about the lack of sex education in our school and in high schools everywhere. Being a teenager is a confusing time. Our bodies are changing. Our emotions are changing. We're starting to date. We're becoming curious about our sexuality. And yet, for some weird reason, sex education in most schools seems to start and stop in fifth grade. Fifth grade! It's like, "Okay, we're going to teach you about this in fifth grade when you're ten or eleven, but then you'll have to figure it out from there." And they always separate the boys and girls in those classes, so neither sex has much of an idea of what the other goes through. The attitude is, "Well, a boy isn't a girl, so why does he need to know what goes on with her body?" Here's one reason: how am I supposed to explain to my boyfriend what endo is and what it does to me and how it may affect our relationship when he can't even comprehend what my period is?

And when they tell a fifth-grade girl that cramping during her period is a normal part of having her period, that's fine, but they also need to explain that there is a threshold; too much pain is not normal. Though they probably don't know to tell her that because they have no idea what endo is or what it can do to a girl. And they don't know that because nobody will talk about a girl's period like they should. It's a vicious cycle that has to stop.

My school told me that with such a rigorous curriculum already, there isn't time to mix in that kind of education. You know what I told them? Figure it out. No girl at my alma mater or any other school should be forced to go through what I went through.

Over the years, I've talked a lot publicly and privately about what endo did to me, but I wish I had publicly talked about it even more in the beginning, especially when the symptoms were occurring. Maybe I would have figured it out sooner. In any case, I know I'm young and fortunate to be where I am today, especially when so many women much older than I have been suffering for decades. I hope that I've given you the confidence to get the help you need now while you're young and the confidence once you are well to pay this forward. There are millions of girls like you who don't have the knowledge about endo that you have right now, and they don't know where to turn. Get yourself well, and then help them. It's going to take a team effort to beat this disease, and we need you on this team.

III

Ways to Treat (and Not Treat) Endo

There is no better way to remove endometriosis than through the laparoscopic deep-excision surgery that I've performed thousands of times. But sometimes surgery isn't the best option, especially if you're young. Know the options available to you before jumping into surgery, and also know what you shouldn't do to try to manage it. Some "remedies" can do more harm than good.

CHAPTER 9

Diet and Nutrition

There is nothing more important to our health than what we put into our bodies. Good nutrition is the basis for healthy living and avoiding or combating numerous diseases.

If you have endo, what you eat isn't going to make it disappear, and what you eat may not prevent you from having to one day have surgery. But the food you consume could slow the endo's growth and prevent many symptoms, such as pain, diarrhea, constipation, and bloating, from continuously interrupting your life. And that's some important knowledge to have, especially when you are a young teen trying to understand and navigate your way through this disease.

You know by now that endo, like probably every disease, is not a one-size-fits-all disease. It affects everyone differently. The symptoms can be different, the ages at which you can get it vary, the remedies can be diverse. The same goes for what each person should or shouldn't eat. If I'm speaking to ten endo patients at once, I cannot tell them all to eat this or not eat that. It's going to require some experimentation on their part to see how their bodies react. However, it helps for everyone to have a starting point.

The key to keeping your endo calm and regulating any symptoms is to avoid anything that can cause inflammation. Just as burning the endo with a laser can cause inflammation, so can some of the foods you eat.

At one of my medical conferences several years ago, one of the speakers, Kimberly Smith Niezgoda, gave an outstanding presentation on nutrition that is on my endofound.org website and that I still refer to today. Some inflammatory foods she mentioned included dairy, white sugar, anything deep-fried or processed, red meat, alcohol, wheat, trans fats, and common cooking oils. She also said that gluten, coffee, and tobacco can cause problems.

But you don't have to eat like a rabbit to avoid endo symptoms. Giving up tobacco and sugar and deep-fried foods is going to be good for you no matter what. But start by trying to cut one item at a time to see if you can figure out exactly what is causing your issues so that you know what to avoid without having to guess. Think of the last time you had a symptom and what you may have eaten prior to it. If it was dairy, give up just dairy for a while to see what happens. If that doesn't solve it, then try something else. Continue experimenting until you have a breakthrough.

Some anti-inflammatory foods that Kimberly discussed that you can add to your regular diet include dark-green leafy vegetables, eggs, organic meats, blueberries, pineapple, broccoli, cauliflower, sweet potatoes, extra-virgin olive oil, papaya, pistachios, walnuts, almonds, chestnuts, wild salmon, coconut oil, shiitake mushrooms, green tea, beets, sprouts, legumes, dates, figs, apricots, cumin, and turmeric.

Everything I've listed as being inflammatory and anti-inflammatory is likely not new information to anyone who has taken general health classes in school or who has paid attention to any health studies in recent decades. But the challenge is to put a sound diet plan into action.

Unfortunately, our taste buds often come ahead of good nutrition, which is one reason why we don't always eat as well as we should. Another reason may be that we are conditioned to eat and drink a certain way based on our lifestyles, what our parents grew up eating, or what social pressures we may be under. For example, if we're running from one after-school activity to another, fast food might be commonplace because of its convenience. If our parents still believe that the four food groups of meat, dairy, bread, and fruits and vegetables that they learned about in school are the basis for healthy eating, and if they are the ones who cook dinner each night, that may be how we eat too. If we are attending a lot of school parties with alcohol, social pressures may cause us to drink.

But you have to find the mental strength to take charge of your own body and what you put in it. It may require you the day before a game to prepare a healthy meal that you can take on the go, or it may require you to teach yourself how to cook so that you can make your own healthy dinners, or you may have to avoid some social functions if the temptations are too much.

Listen to your body. If you have endo symptoms, take steps to change your diet. It could take some time to figure out what works and what doesn't, but if you can find the right combination and reduce or even eliminate some of your symptoms, you'll feel much better.

My Name Is Tanya

"When I was fifteen, I figured out that what I ate mattered, especially during my period."

My mother and grandmother didn't talk much to me about my period when I got my first one at the age of twelve. It was painful with heavy bleeding, but that didn't seem too out of the ordinary to them. It continued that way until I was about fifteen; I just assumed that's how it was supposed to be.

My periods became more intense with cramping and bloating when I turned twenty-three. The doctor's assessment and remedy were simple: my hormones were changing, and I needed to take a stronger dose of Aleve. At twenty-four, my bowels became difficult, to put it mildly. To put it not-so-mildly, I felt like all of my organs were trying to push their way out of my body. At twenty-seven, the symptoms were unbearable—the cramps, the bloating, the bowels, the nausea. I did my own research, and though I'd never heard of the disease before, I concluded that I might have endometriosis.

When I went to the doctor, she ordered a sonogram. As it was being done, I vividly remember the look on the technician's face. The best way to describe it in a word would be "alarming." She kept walking in and out of the room without saying anything to me. I knew something serious was wrong. When I returned to the doctor for the results, she said she was confident that I had endo, yet she was very casual about it. Whatever spooked the technician didn't spook her. She told me she'd put me on birth control and that I would be fine.

I should have trusted the technician's facial expressions.

I went on the pill, but it didn't work. I bled all the time, including through ovulation. Sex was painful. Relationships were suffering. I had to set my alarm to go off early enough each morning so that I had time to deal with the vomiting and diarrhea and cramping before I left the house, which would give me a solid hour to get to work before I'd relive all three again.

When I was thirty, I had laser surgery. The doctor found that one of my ovaries and the back side of my uterus were plastered to my colon. She said to me, "At this point, you can't even afford to eat a bagel." The surgery was, in essence, unsuccessful, and for the next four years I popped Aleve like it was candy. The previous symptoms not only started again but I was now experiencing fatigue and what felt like major indigestion. During workouts I was gasping for air during the most basic movements. Walking up steps became such a chore I felt like I was going to pass out. Then I noticed a crackling in my chest, leading me to believe I might have pneumonia.

If only that had been it.

A chest X-ray revealed that my right lung had collapsed. I was sent to the ER where they inserted a tube to open the lung. They sent me home, but less than twenty-four hours later the lung had collapsed again. I returned to the ER where the doctor, who had some knowledge of endometriosis, suspected that's what I might have. When he did surgery to fix my lung, his suspicion was correct. My diaphragm was covered in lesions, which are what collapsed my lung.

While I recovered from the surgery, and with an urgency to address the endo that was still inside of me, I did more research and found Dr. Seckin, who performed a nine-hour operation. Along with all the endo, he had to remove my left ovary, my belly button, and a foot of my colon—otherwise known as a bowel resection. He also had to reconstruct my belly and bladder. For the first time in twenty years, I felt "normal" again.

With my story coming after the chapter on the importance of good nutrition when you have endo, you're probably wondering how any of what I've said relates to that. Well, you may have noticed in the beginning of my story that I skipped about eight years, from when I was fifteen until I was twenty-three. Things were definitely bad for me then; there was a lot of heavy bleeding during my period, but the pain was manageable. The reason for that is that when I was fifteen, I figured out that what I ate mattered, especially during my period. I would give up certain foods about a week prior to having it, which made my monthly suffering bearable.

I made the connection one night when my mom made meat loaf and I didn't feel very well afterward. I started paying attention to other foods I consumed and was amazed at what I learned. My bloating normally occurred after I had dairy. When I ate bread, I could count on being constipated. Red meat of any kind, meat loaf or otherwise, was difficult to digest and made me gassy. I also cut out caffeine and sugar. Changing my diet before and during my period is what got me through those years. I can't imagine how much worse I would have felt had I not done that.

Why did my diet not help as much after I turned twenty-three? Considering the endo made its way all the way to my diaphragm, I assume it just overpowered my entire insides and nothing was going to stop it. But who knows, maybe the diet still did help during that time, just not as effectively. If only I had been diagnosed with endo during those teen years while my diet had the symptoms somewhat under control, maybe I could have avoided all of the agony I went through in my twenties and thirties.

Today, post-surgery, I've completely cut out dairy, red meat, and gluten, and I don't miss any of them. I also buy more organic foods, and if I have alcohol, it's only wine, and I stop at two glasses.

The way I ate during my teen years and the way I eat today may not be what's best for you. But know that your diet can make a difference. Take the time to discover how it can make a difference for you. Endo is bad enough as it is. If you can slow it down and limit your symptoms by sacrificing some foods you love or trying new ones, it's well worth it.

CHAPTER 10

Physical Activity

Any physical activity that gets you moving and having fun is good for you, both mentally and physically, no matter your fitness level. When you have endo, exercise isn't going to diminish the disease in the same way it can directly affect other conditions, like lowering your blood pressure or level of cholesterol. But exercise can help to balance your hormone levels, which, when imbalanced, can contribute to developing endo. The right and regular exercise can help you manage your weight and the pain that endo causes.

Dr. Jim Palmer is a well-respected physical therapist in New York City who has spoken at my medical conferences about the link between endo and exercise. I will let him share some of his expertise with you, which is quite enlightening for anybody who is dealing with any condition that has grounded them in some way.

"As a physical therapist, I've worked with many teenage girls who have pain—hip pain, back pain, pelvic pain, both long and short term—caused by various conditions or injuries. In the same way that you need to find the right primary care doctor or gynecologist who will listen to your needs and help you get the results you are looking for, you should partner with the right physical therapist to help you treat your pain. Helping you reduce or completely overcome your pain is what we do. Your physical therapist must be willing to find the root cause of your pain and provide you with exercise-based solutions to solve the problems you are dealing with. Your therapist should design a program that will help you get back to activities that are most important to you."

After discussing your pain with you, Dr. Palmer will explain the power of attitude and knowing the difference between good pain and bad pain.

"If you're in pain from endo, you are usually limited in doing activities that you enjoy or need to do, such as moving around the house, sitting for long periods in class, walking for long stretches, or participating in clubs and sports at school. As a result of your pain, you spend more time in bed or on the couch. This makes your body stiffer and weaker, which contributes to having even more pain. That inactivity could cause other health issues to develop. The right physical therapist will teach you how to take control of your pain and stop letting pain take over you. You must say to yourself, "It makes me happy to go out with friends, so I'm going to find a way to do that." Or, "It makes me happy when I'm playing this sport or working with this club, so I must find a way to continue playing or participating." It' not easy to do, especially if you have been dealing with pain for a long time, but your mind is very powerful. What you believe becomes your reality.

"I also teach my clients to understand the difference between good pain and bad pain. If you're doing a physical activity that causes soreness or your body to be a little tired, that's good, appropriate pain, even if that soreness lasts a couple days. This soreness and tiredness will improve as your body grows stronger. But if the physical activity you're doing causes your endo to flare up with sharp pains to your stomach or pelvic area, then you should stop doing it. That's bad, inappropriate pain, and doing it more because you think you should be tough and fight through it isn't going to help you. My suggestion would be to decrease the intensity of that exercise or try a different exercise all together. Everyone is different, so you have to find the activities that make your body and mind feel the best."

Dr. Palmer also suggests that every endo patient should pay attention to their posture and breathing.

"With regard to posture, it is common for girls with endo to double over while standing, sitting, or lying in bed because of pain. Doubling over for long periods puts a lot of pressure on their abdominal and pelvic regions, which causes more pain. For this reason, I teach my patients to sit straight and stand tall. You will decrease pressure on your abdomen and pelvis, improving your pain.

"Taking smooth, deep, comfortable breaths will help, too. We'll oftentimes hear people say, 'Remember to breathe.' Breathing is natural, but sometimes we don't realize that we tense up because of pain and are breathing much less, which will only exacerbate the pain. Knowing how breathing affects your pelvic floor can influence your endo. Your diaphragm, a muscle within your ribcage that helps your lungs expand and contract, is connected to your pelvic floor. When you hold your breath or only take shallow breaths because of pain, you hold your diaphragm tight and your pelvic floor won't move. This can contribute to having worse endo pain. However, if you breathe deep to the sound of relaxing music or while being still with your eyes closed, your diaphragm will move, causing your pelvic floor to relax and improve your pain.

"Another concept I teach my patients is to 'control their controllables.' What do I mean by this? There are things we can control in life and things we cannot control. For example, I cannot control the weather. But if it is raining outside, I can choose to wear a jacket, boots, and carry an umbrella. I cannot control the weather, but I can control what I wear so that I am dry and comfortable. In the same vein, I cannot control that I have endo, but I can choose to make healthier choices to improve my mental and physical state. I can choose to go out and be active with friends. I can choose to go for a walk, go to a yoga class, or play a sport to improve my fitness. I can choose to avoid candy and soda, which contribute to obesity and diabetes. I can choose to eat vegetables and fruits so that my body has good energy and heals better when I'm sick. I feel that this is important for endo patients to practice. You do not have control over how or when you got endo. You *can* control how you manage your endo pain through regular physical activity and exercise."

Dr. Palmer says people ask him all the time, "What is the best exercise for me?"

"As a physical therapist I know that there are specific exercises for specific injuries. "I think that when it comes to my endo patients, it's about finding the best combination of exercise and activity that improves their pain and that is enjoyable to do. Finding exercise and activities that you truly enjoy are so important when managing endo; if you enjoy something, you will keep doing it. Some examples of exercise that can be helpful to endo patients are yoga, strength training, and sports play. By partnering with the right physical therapist, you can determine what is the best combination of exercise and activity for you.

"Yoga may be my favorite exercise for endo patients because of its focus on deep breathing, strength, and flexibility training. Yoga is usually performed in a calming environment, which can help reduce mental stress that is common in endo patients. The deep breathing will improve your diaphragm and pelvic floor's ability to move, which can improve pain. Holding and moving through yoga poses will improve the strength and flexibility of your legs, arms, and core. The stronger and more flexible you are will help your body's posture and improve pain. All yoga classes and instructors are different, so it's about finding the right fit for you and your body.

"Strength training is not just for guys, it's important for girls, too. Don't worry about developing big and bulky muscles. Your genetic makeup is different, so you will grow lean and fit. Having a stronger core, arms, and legs, is essential for carrying bags, climbing steps, walking, squatting to the floor, and running around. Having more lean muscle will help your body stay at a healthy weight and fight off diabetes. Strength training can be performed using your body weight through squats, push-ups, and planks. Or, at the gym, you can use machines, exercise balls, and weights. Have your physical therapist show you how to start strength training safely.

"Sports are also a great way to meet friends who enjoy being active and have a common goal. Your body will grow strong from playing the sport of your choice. There are team-oriented sports such as basketball, softball, field hockey, soccer, lacrosse, and rowing. Or you may try sports that are based more on your individual performance, such as running, swimming, and ballet. When you join the sport you enjoy playing the most and meet people you enjoy spending your time with, you will feel the greatest benefit.

"If none of these activities are really your thing, then try going for a walk, hike, or bike ride. Again, be active daily and have fun by yourself or with friends and family. After a few weeks of exercise and activity, the initial soreness and tiredness that your body experiences should be gone, and you will start to see changes. You may feel stronger and more flexible, along with improved pain, posture, and stress levels. By teaming with the right physical therapist, you will have a professional guiding you through your journey. There will be days that your body will feel amazing, and days that your pain comes back. The key is to keep moving forward, making good decisions, and taking control over your life."

My Name Is Brandilee

"I honored my body by doing exactly what it needed."

I've experienced endo pain pretty much my entire life. I had my first period in fifth grade, but the pain started well before that. It was always debilitating and forced me to miss a lot of school. It got worse in high school and college, and I did the tour of doctors that many endo patients do. There was the one who told me that I simply had bad periods and had to find a way to deal with it. There was the one who said birth control would work. It didn't. And, of course, there was the one who insisted that the pain was all in my head. Finally, when I was twenty-four, I found a doctor who did excision surgery. Today, eight years later, I still have some pain, but I feel much better than I did before the operation.

How do I keep that pain in check?

Yoga.

I started yoga when I was twenty-two; it was trendy and a good way to stay in shape. I decided to take it a step further two years later by signing up for a course on how to teach yoga. I was excited about it, though the timing was bad. The first class was just six weeks after my surgery, and my body was still in recovery mode. I went anyway and, as expected, I struggled. I could hardly do a sit-up, let alone go through this fast-paced class.

But it turned out to be the best thing that could have ever happened to me.

Being in that vulnerable position forced me to talk about my endometriosis. I had no choice but to tell my instructors why I wasn't participating like everyone else, and why I was doing restorative poses when I was supposed to be doing a fast class. That led me to tell my classmates about it. It was the first time in my life that I had been so open about my condition, and it was also the first time that I had truly listened to my body. I didn't abuse my body by trying to keep up with everyone else and make it do something it couldn't. I honored my body by doing exactly what it needed.

It was then when I noticed the beneficial connection between endo and yoga, when my endo and yoga journeys became one.

I practice yoga for an hour a day about five times a week. The primary purposes of yoga are to relieve tension in the body and relax the muscles. So, when you have cramps from endo, these poses that you do through yoga target those cramps to give you relief. During the process, it also puts your mind in a good place. You've read plenty of stories already about how endo messes with your mind. Yoga helps you to create that mind and body connection. If you are able to relax yourself physically, it also eases the burden of mental stress.

If you're at all intimidated by trying yoga, there are a couple things I may be able to share with you to ease your concerns.

The first is that yoga is something that can be done by anyone of any age at any time and anywhere. With all of the struggles I had as far back as elementary school, I wish I had been introduced to yoga then; I can picture a younger version of me embracing the discipline. I also wish, after I had started doing yoga in my early twenties, that I hadn't avoided going to classes on days that the endo pain was flaring up. I missed several, and it did me no good to stay home doing nothing and let the disease be in charge. I enjoyed yoga a lot, so I should have participated in whatever way I could have and not worried about what I couldn't do.

The second is that yoga doesn't have to be done at the high level that you may envision it. I think when a lot of people think of yoga, they think of women bending all over the place and basically levitating. You don't have to be balancing on one finger to be a yogi. In fact, even if you can't get out of bed, there are yoga poses that you can do from there, such as the butterfly pose. Many poses don't require you to be very physical and on a mat.

I did earn my yoga certification when I took that course right after my surgery. I not only teach today but I have created classes specifically for women with endometriosis. Aside from yoga, I also like to bike and box. Endo at times creates anger and frustration within me, as it does in everyone with the disease, and I've found the serenity in yoga to be the best thing for me to control that rage. But pushing pedals through bike trails or getting in a few punches every now and then doesn't hurt either.

Endo wants to control your body and mind. Don't let it. Find exercises that physically and mentally feel good, and do them regularly. Whether it's a very light workout or an intense one, just do something to stay active. Every bit helps.

CHAPTER 11

Birth Control Pills

Because of its name, or because of what you may have been taught by your parents, religion, or sex education class, you may think of birth control pills as having just one purpose: to prevent pregnancy. Actually, the main function of birth control pills is to prevent ovulation (when eggs are released from the ovaries), and therefore secondarily prevent pregnancy. So, yes, they are most often prescribed to those who are or plan to be sexually active.

But that's not their only purpose.

I have prescribed birth control pills, commonly called "the pill," to girls who are not sexually active. Sometimes they're as young as twelve or thirteen and don't intend on having intercourse for years. I prescribe it because I know the girls have endo and need some relief from the symptoms, and the pill can provide this.

The pill is a mild hormonal medicine that will regulate your period and suppress the increased effect of estrogen in the uterus. Taking the pill can lessen the bleeding that you may have during your period. It may lessen the pain caused by menstrual cramps. It may cause you to have fewer periods and/or shorten the length of your periods, which would in turn reduce the bleeding and pain during those periods.

Some parents of girls who may have endo, or the girls themselves, will still say that there is no way they will consider the pill because of their religious beliefs. I am perfectly fine with that. No doctor is going to force it upon you. The only point I would make before you completely rule it out is to consider the intent. The reason for the prescription would have nothing whatsoever to do with sexual intercourse. It would be prescribed to enable you to go to school, go to work, be involved in sports and other activities, and maintain your relationships with friends that could otherwise be fractured because of the havoc endo is wreaking on your life. There wouldn't be a person on the planet, outside of me, your parents, and the pharmacist, who would know that I prescribed it to you.

The pill will not make your endo disappear or stop it from spreading. What it can do is shrink an ovarian cyst or slow down the endo's growth process (because the pill would reduce the amount of estrogen produced in your body). It would serve as a suppressant toward endo, much like some other methods (nutrition, exercise, etc.), to make you feel good enough to be able to do the things you need and want to do while you are young. Taking the pill for endo wouldn't be a lot different from someone taking Advil for headaches. If the headaches persist, the Advil may provide temporary relief, but the root of the problem will eventually have to be addressed.

The pill does not work for everyone, which is why you and your doctor would need to monitor how it affects you as soon as it is prescribed. I would first put you on it just during your period. If that doesn't suppress your pain, I would put you on it every day. The pill is not an addictive drug like narcotics, so there is nothing to worry about in that respect. The pill, however, may not reduce any of your symptoms, which could mean the endo is already so deep and widespread that it needs to be attacked in a different manner. The pill can also cause side effects, such as weight gain or depression, which is why monitoring is essential.

You've already read several stories from my patients who said the pill was prescribed and didn't work for them. For others it will work. There are different types and brands of the pill, so it may take some experimentation to figure out what works best for you, if any.

Miranda, whose story you read about empowerment, was sixteen when she had back pain that her doctor would determine was caused by ovarian cysts. The cysts, she said, resolved themselves, but the back pain continued to hamper her. Her family also had a history of endo.

"The pain alarmed us because my mom had endo and had to have a hysterectomy seven years ago," Miranda said. "And my aunt, my dad's sister, had it a long time ago. Her case was really bad. She ended up sterile and still has complications today."

Suspecting the cause of the back pain could be endo, Miranda's doctor wanted to put her on the pill with the hope that it would provide her some relief. But her mother knew, given endo's prevalence in the family, the pill would not solve the underlying problem. That's when the family found me, and I did surgery on Miranda. After the surgery, I put her on birth control to give her body some rest from her periods. It served the purpose for which it was prescribed.

"It's working well," Miranda said. "It's preventing ovulation and my periods, and I'm not in any pain."

Miranda said being prescribed the pill was okay with her and her family.

"We don't see it as being wrong," Miranda said. "Plus, I'm not sexually active; I'm using it purely for other medical purposes. So it wasn't an issue for me or my family at all."

One final note regarding the purpose of the pill and pregnancy, a perspective that many people don't consider: Endometriosis is the leading cause of infertility in females. I have had countless patients who couldn't get pregnant, who have spent hundreds of thousands of dollars on fertility treatments, or who had miscarriages as a result of endo. But, after surgery to remove the endo, the majority of them were able to have children. So, if taking the pill as a teenager can slow down the endo's growth and prevent it from spreading to places such as your ovaries and fallopian tubes until you are older and in a better position for surgery, being on the pill at such a young age could be the reason why you stay fertile and are able to have children later in life. In that case, the pill would not have been working as a deterrent against pregnancy, but as a catalyst for it.

My Name Is Kim

"You have to listen to your own body, and if the pill can help you, you should consider giving it a go."

In ten years I went through three gastroenterologists, four dietitians, one naturopath, two gynecologists, two CT scans, two colonoscopies, two pain specialists, one psychiatrist, two psychologists, one endoscopy, one sigmoidoscopy, six ultrasounds, one MRI, and four emergency room visits.

There were also numerous blood tests, doctor visits, medication prescriptions, pregnancy tests, urine tests, STD tests, and countless hours of being poked and prodded, told that it's in my head, told that it's from stress, told that it's from food, and told that it's all my fault.

And I can't forget the kidney, urinary, and bacterial infections, along with diarrhea, constipation, decreased appetite, weight loss, rectal bleeding, cramps, nausea, gas, bloating, depression, anxiety, heavy periods with harsh pain, pain that traveled down my legs, pain before and during and after urination, pain before and during and after bowel movements, pain during intercourse, pain when I ate, pain when I didn't eat, and pain every other moment of every day without an answer.

Are you exhausted yet?

This was my normal before surgery with Dr. Seckin.

Actually, this is the normal for many endo patients, including those whose stories you've read so far. I wanted you to see it all in one list to get the scope of it. Hopefully your symptoms haven't reached this point, and hopefully you won't come close.

The only thing that consistently helped me during those ten years and continues to help me today post-surgery is the pill.

I was fortunate that my parents were open to me taking birth control, realizing that it had medicinal uses beyond preventing pregnancy. The pregnancy part wasn't relevant to me since I wasn't sexually active. I was fourteen when it was first prescribed to me for my painful periods, and it worked well. It was a low dosage that enabled me to go to school and participate in extracurriculars and do things with my friends. I initially experimented with four or five different kinds to see what worked best for my body. I got off one I was taking to see if the bloating I was feeling was a side effect of the pill or from something else. I also tried one that prevented my period from happening at all, but I decided that felt too unnatural. I eventually settled on one that had the least side effects, and I chose to stop my period every other month to lessen the symptoms. The pain was more noticeable the six months I did have my period, but it wasn't enough to stop me from living my life.

When I was in high school, I had some friends who were having really bad periods. I don't know whether they had endo or not, but they were struggling each month. When I told them I used to have the same thing but was fine now that I was on the pill, they were shocked.

"Oh my gosh," they would say to me. "My parents would never believe that was the reason I want it. I'd have to go behind their backs to get it."

And some of them did. They were good kids, but they had to do what they had to do to survive.

If you're a parent of a girl with endo symptoms and a doctor suggests trying birth control, I think you should give it a chance. It has nothing to do with sex. Nothing. It has to do with your daughter being able to function day to day, and the pill is one of the simplest, most private, non-invasive remedies there is. It may not work for her once she tries it, and she will be able to figure that out pretty quickly by how her body reacts. If that's the case, she'll want to stop using it and try something else, but I believe it's worth a shot.

For girls who are in as much pain as most of the women in this book were when they were young teens, desperately trying to find some way to make it stop, I say this: if your parents say no to the pill and offer no other solutions, and if they tell you that your pain is normal and part of being a woman, do your best to state your case with facts and statistics and stories such as mine that could sway their opinions. If they still won't listen, I would suggest that you go to a doctor or clinic and get the pill yourself.

That's my sole opinion, and I know that may sound controversial; I am not one to advocate for someone to go behind their parents' backs. But I know what the pain and other symptoms are like. Tens of millions of women around the world know what they're like. And even more women and men than that have absolutely no idea what it's like because they have not had and never will have endo. But you can't listen to those people if they are going to deny you an effective treatment because of their lack of education on the subject. You have to listen to your own body, and if you believe the pill can help you, you should consider giving it a go.

I have been on the pill since my surgery, and I continue to skip every other period. My period pain is pretty much nonexistent. When I do feel some, it's easily manageable. Since endometriosis is a chronic disease, it can certainly grow back. The hope is that if I stay on the pill, which my body has been receptive to since I was fourteen, any endo that tries to grow back will do so at a snail's pace and will not affect me in any glaring ways like it did for the past ten years.

CHAPTER 12

Excision Surgery Is Gold

Remember my four steps to determining for sure if you have endo? They are a clinical exam, testing (such as a sonogram or an MRI), surgery, and the inspection of the tissue under a microscope. I also pay careful attention to a patient's clinical history.

In more advanced cases of endometriosis, I would have a good idea if a patient has endo by the end of our first consultation. Even the way a patient with advanced endometriosis enters the room, positions herself in the chair across from me as she sits down, and/ or changes positions a number of times during our discussion is revealing. In other words, I would be able to "see" an advanced endometriosis patient's pain. I would have further confirmation when she tells me her symptoms and any anecdotal evidence of her pain and discomfort. The clinical exam and testing would just about confirm it.

However, endo is harder to immediately diagnose in young women and girls. In adolescence, the inflammation associated with endo is still young and the scar tissues are not yet hardened. As a result, a pelvic exam would not confirm endometriosis because of the consequent lack of tenderness. Furthermore, because it might be the first time this young woman is at a gynecologist, the patient may not be as comfortable with a pelvic exam and endovaginal sonogram. As a result, it could be difficult to tell whether the discomfort from a manual exam is due to disease-related tenderness. However, it is nonetheless crucial for young women to remain aware of the possibility that not only could they have this disease but they may require surgery. So, why not immediately remove the endo through surgery rather than try to experiment with nutrition or exercises, or go on birth control? For a few reasons. First, the body of a young person doesn't need to be put through a surgical procedure if there are less invasive methods that manage symptoms to try first. Second, surgery has risks and complications. It is important to establish a confirmation of sustained symptoms of pain, and to not rush the decision to pursue surgical treatment. A patient should exhaust all symptom management options before she pursues surgical treatment.

If a specialist determines that surgery is necessary, I want you to know the different surgery options, because not all endo surgeries are the same. In fact, they are quite different. Some, which I'll discuss in the next chapter, can have long-term devastating results.

Laparoscopic deep-excision surgery, which is what I call the "gold standard" of endo surgery and is the only method I use, enables me to perform surgery in the most precise manner possible. I use cold scissors to literally cut out the endo (hot scissors use electrical energy, whereas cold scissors are manual). I then repair any organs onto which the endo has adhered, such as the ovaries, bowel, and bladder. Because endometriosis deforms a patient's pelvic organs, it is imperative to restore the disfigured anatomy. Reconstruction consists of meticulous tissue handling, precise bleeding control, and artful suturing. This expertise comes with years of experience. We desperately need more surgeons in this country and around the world who can perform this type of operation—the more doctors who can, the better it will be for women everywhere.

I was introduced to this method more than thirty years ago, yet few surgeons today know how to do it. It requires significant study, knowledge, time, precision, dexterity, and patience, all of which can often conflict with the way our education and health-care systems today are designed. So many doctors are taught to be expeditious, to get patients in and out as soon as possible. Insurance companies will even dictate this. While laparoscopic deep-excision surgery does not necessarily require a long hospital stay, and while it is a safe surgery to have, it is not routine and cannot be rushed.

When I say it is "laparoscopic," that means I use an instrument known as a laparoscope, a long, thin tube with a telescopic lens, multiple light sources, and a miniature video camera. That and all instruments I use are inserted into a tiny incision in the patient's naval, no more than five to ten millimeters in length, while the patient is under anesthesia. A few similar incisions may be made in the same area. The incisions I cut are very small; one, for example, goes through the belly button and is so tiny, there is consequently a hardly-visible scar. The instruments serve as extensions of my hands. A large monitor is set up across from me, on the other side of the patient, so I can clearly see the patient's internal organs. As I watch the monitor, I move my instrument meticulously, pixel by pixel, to cut out every speck of the disease with the cold scissors. A surgery will last three to four hours on average, and sometimes up to five or ten hours. Given its complexity, few surgeons have been trained, or want to take the time to be trained, to perform this procedure.

Laparoscopic deep-excision surgery removes the endo from every organ down to the root, as I describe in the "weed" analogy. Another way I describe it to my patients is using the analogy of an iceberg. Picture the peak of an iceberg (the endometriosis) protruding above the water (an organ in the body). If I shave the top of the iceberg that I can see above the water, which other types of surgeries do, it may appear like I've gotten it all, but the largest and most dense portion of the iceberg remains below water, left to continue growing and flourishing. Deep-excision surgery permanently removes the entire iceberg and provides the most pain relief.

A patient's recovery period will vary, though most of my patients go home within twenty-four hours. How long a patient is out of school or work could range from a week to a month—every person is different.

I can never promise a patient that her pain will drop to a specific level; no doctor can guarantee a precise result. But most will find the pain reduced so considerably that they can quickly reclaim their lives. If it doesn't go away as much as expected or hoped, another surgery could be necessary. Sometimes the endo is so deep or widespread that I can't do it all at once, for fear of nerve damage or what is known as "surgeon's fatigue." Nine or ten hours is about as long as I can go in a surgery. If it requires much longer, a second surgery would be necessary.

So now you know what I do and what I believe every endo surgeon should do, if surgery appears to be necessary. But if so many people don't know what endo is, what are the chances of you being recommended to this type of surgery that so few doctors know how to do? Almost zero. Which means if they do suggest you have surgery, it's usually going to be a type of surgery that I strongly do *not* recommend, as you'll read in the next chapter.

My Name Is Rachel

*"My worst days today are better than
my best days before my surgery."*

I was a junior in high school, seventeen years old, and it was Halloween. My girlfriends and I went to school dressed as football players,
and we wanted to take some pictures in the hallway before class.

They did, but I couldn't.

I was crouched in the hall corner, crying from the most intense
menstrual cramps I'd ever felt. After several minutes, I was finally
able to scrape my body off the floor and drag myself to the nurse's
office. She gave me an Advil and sent me to class. When it didn't
kick in after a few hours, I called my mom to pick me up.

"I don't know what to do," I cried. "I can't stand up."

"I can come get you," Mom said, "but then you can't go out tonight."

Not go out on Halloween? That wasn't happening. I hobbled to
the store during lunch and bought more Advil. I popped four into
my mouth, returned to school, and pushed forward.

From that day on, the first two days of my period each month
were debilitating. Every woman and doctor told me it was "normal." Not being able to walk was normal? Waking in bed to find
my clothes and sheets soiled in blood was normal? It didn't seem
possible, but how could everyone be wrong?

Like many girls with this disease who don't know what's happening to them, I studied and worked and socialized through the
pain, hiding it at every turn. It negatively affected my grades, my
job, and my relationships, and the worst part was that I could never
explain it to anybody. Because nobody could explain it to me.

When I was twenty-one, I saw a TV commercial for endometriosis. I'd never heard the word before, but the symptoms they described appeared to match mine.

"Mom, I think this is what I have," I told her.

"No, I'm sure you don't," she said in passing.

My mom and dad are my rocks. They are compassionate and loving parents. But how could I expect them to believe a commercial over my doctors, who insisted my symptoms were nothing out of the ordinary? As much as my pain didn't make sense to me, I understood my parents' reasoning. So, I continued with the Advil, which sometimes worked and sometimes didn't.

When I was about twenty-three, more symptoms had developed, including pain in my lower back, legs, and stomach. When I told my gynecologist, he used that word "normal" again, told me to up my Advil dosage to six at a time, and then he left the room.

Yes, six at a time.

That many at once caused stomach ulcers, so I stopped taking it. When the stomach pain continued, I was diagnosed with celiac disease. Around that same time, my period had gone from being insanely painful two days a month to five days a month, sometimes longer. I went to a different gynecologist, a woman, counting on her to figure this out. Her solution was to prescribe me a giant bottle of Percocet. I knew Percocet was, unfortunately, a highly addictive narcotic, but she said it was that or nothing. I chose nothing.

Over the next two years I would be put on a gluten-free diet, be given meds for nausea, have painful bowel movements and throbbing migraines, and land in the emergency room twice for what doctors diagnosed as kidney infections. The symptoms for a kidney infection are similar to those of endo, but my kidneys weren't infected. I would later learn that was their go-to diagnosis for something they couldn't legitimately diagnose.

All of this led to depression and anxiety. When my period was about to happen each month, I knew the hell that was waiting on the horizon. And when it arrived, it was torture. I couldn't take it anymore. I went back to my gynecologist, determined to convince her that something was gravely wrong. I told her about that commercial I'd seen five years earlier.

"I think I have endometriosis," I told her.

She thought about it for a moment and then said two words that, for the first time in ten years, gave me hope and made me believe I would be taken seriously.

"That's possible," she said.

She prescribed me birth control pills, which would regulate my menstrual cycle and hopefully stifle the pain, but it didn't work. That's when she suggested surgery and recommended me to Dr. Seckin. Soon after my meeting with him, convinced that I had endo, he went in and cut out forty lesions. Forty! And thirty-eight of them came back positive for endo! He also had to remove my appendix because it was practically encased in the disease.

"You can't imagine the agony she's been in all of these years," he said to my parents after surgery.

When I was leaving the hospital the day after my operation and he came to see me for the second time, I burst into tears. He told me not to cry as he hugged me, but I couldn't help it. They were happy tears. I already felt better than I had in a decade. I knew he'd given me my life back.

Please don't lose sight of my messages to you. You do not have to come to New York City to see Dr. Seckin; there are other doctors who can do what he does. You may not even need surgery, especially if you are very young and your symptoms have just started. But please know two things: nobody can help you until you are properly diagnosed, and once you are diagnosed, you have to get the right treatment. For me, after ten years, the right treatment was surgery. And not just any surgery, but laparoscopic deep-excision surgery.

I wish that I had known about endo ten years ago. I wish my pediatrician or school nurse or gynecologist or mom or friends would have known more. I tell my friends about endo today and most of them still don't know what it is. Nobody should ever tell you that pain beyond measure is normal. Nobody should ever tell you that it's part of becoming a woman. And no doctor should ever prescribe you narcotics.

Once you do determine that it's endo you have, don't think that all surgeries are the same, because they aren't. Some can harm you more than they can help. Also know that your pain will likely never be completely gone, because endo is a chronic disease. But the person I was before surgery and person I am today—I can't compare the two. My worst days today are better than my best days before my surgery. When I do feel pain now, it's manageable. I no longer have to worry about not being able to physically do something. Plans I make with friends and family are no longer tentative.

In other words, I'm living my life again, as I deserve. And you deserve the same. Don't ever doubt that.

CHAPTER 13

What Laser Surgery Will Do to You

Using a laser to treat endometriosis, to some surgeons, is like playing a video game. Their surgical tool superficially sprays electrical energy or light energy onto the tips of the endo (the parts of the icebergs "above water"), burning off those tips with each hit. The endo they can't see (the parts of the icebergs "below water") remains behind. The results are largely devastating for the patient, who will feel the symptoms return as the endo starts to grow again. The patient will also probably have more pain the second time around from the scar tissue that the laser left behind.

There are two laser methods doctors use today to eliminate endometriosis tissues that I do not support. These two methods are electric fulguration (also known as cautery) and laser ablation surgery. Electric fulguration uses heat from an electrical current to destroy endometriosis tissue. But this procedure chars the tissues, which turn black. As a result, electric fulguration surgery only creates additional scarring in lieu of treatment.

The second is laser ablation surgery. Instead of electricity, light energy is used. This process is also called laser vaporization surgery. In laser ablation surgery, light energy boils the cells and vaporizes them. Though this procedure sounds cleaner than electric fulguration, the diseased tissue remains under the surface. Again, this method only treats the tip of the iceberg.

Let me be as direct as possible: if your doctor suggests treating your endo through laparoscopic surgery using laser ablation or electric fulguration, grab your things and run out the door as fast as you can. Or, maybe to be more polite, say, "Thank you, but I don't think that type of surgery is for me." And then grab your things and run out the door as fast as you can.

I also want to be just as clear about this: a third method, laparoscopic low-voltage carbon dioxide (CO_2) laser surgery, is similar to the excision surgery I perform with cold scissors. However, for many reasons, the carbon dioxide method is not as precise as the cold scissors, as it will leave behind some burned tissue and can inadvertently perforate major organs. Furthermore, because there is no tissue feedback (feeling of the tissue), a surgeon cannot maneuver the laser beam as you can maneuver scissors with your hand. As a result, significant endometriosis tissue may be left behind, causing incomplete treatment. In my opinion, the CO_2 method is a viable option if laparoscopic deep-excision surgery is not available to you. Just note that many doctors who say they can remove your endo through laparoscopic surgery, not specifying whether it is with cold scissors, electric fulguration, laser ablation, or CO_2 surgery, are generally referring to electric fulguration surgery.

Here are details of some of the significant problems I've mentioned with electric fulguration surgery. First, because electric fulguration surgery cannot get to the root of the endo, the endo stays inside you. If a dandelion weed were endo, using this type of surgery would be like zapping off the yellow flower portion of the dandelion without pulling the entire weed, and expecting the yellow flower to never come back. As long as the root is there, the weed will continue to grow and spread.

Second, the scar tissue left behind by electric fulguration surgery can result in pain as grueling as the pain caused by the endo itself.

Electric fulguration attempts to get rid of an inflammation (the endo) with a burn, which is an inflammation itself. The procedure will leave behind cooked, or inflamed, tissue on top of the already inflamed endometriosis.

Sometimes a patient will enjoy a brief reprieve from the pain immediately after electric fulguration surgery, but not always. And even if she does, she should expect that the pain will eventually return with a vengeance. I would safely say that six out of every ten patients who come to me have had at least one laser ablation surgery or electric fulguration surgery, though most of them have had it done multiple times because their surgeons knew no other way.

Lynn started getting painful periods when she was eleven. By the age of fifteen she had pain every single day that kept her out of school and prevented her from going out with her friends on weekends. When she turned sixteen, she would have three electric fulguration surgeries in ten months. The first one was to remove a cyst and part of her left ovary.

"I recovered quickly and had no pain or pressure for two weeks, but then it all came back," Lynn said. "A CAT scan showed a rupturing cyst. An MRI showed I had deep-infiltrating endo. I was sent to a specialist who did my second surgery. Three weeks to the day after the surgery I was so bloated that I looked pregnant. It got to a point where I was bleeding all the time. I took Percocet, and it did nothing."

Lynn's third surgery was with her OB/GYN.

"That actually made the symptoms a whole lot worse," she said.

She finally found me for her fourth surgery three months later. It would be the last surgery she would need.

"What's crazy is that the specialist who did the second surgery told me that he excised it, but I saw the photos after the surgery and could see the burns. When I questioned him and told him the pain was back, he insisted that it was excised and that it couldn't have returned. He told me that I was depressed and needed physical therapy."

Nobody, especially a sixteen-year-old, should have to have four surgeries in thirteen months when one surgery could have helped her pain.

"I do plan to call the specialist one day to tell him about the surgery I had from Dr. Seckin," Lynn said. "I'll be respectful and not do it out of spite. I just need to educate him more on this disease so that he hopefully doesn't put another girl through this or doubt her when she says the pain is there."

If you've tried short-term remedies that aren't working, such as birth control, a new nutrition regimen, exercise, or medication, surgery may be the way to go. If that's the case, your first option should be the laparoscopic deep-excision surgery with cold scissors. Your second option should be the low-voltage CO_2 laser surgery. And at no time should electric fulguration or laser ablation surgery be an option. If the surgeon says he or she is going to "excise" the endo, learn from Lynn's story and ask how. Excision to me means physically cutting it out. Excision to someone else may mean "removing it" in whatever way they choose, which could be with electric fulguration or laser ablation surgery. And if you think electric fulguration or laser ablation surgery is the only option you have, keep looking. If you have to hold out a little longer until you find that viable option, you will be grateful that you did.

My Name Is Grace

"Believe me when I say you
should not get this kind of surgery. Ever."

I had killer cramps the first day I got my first period, and my pain increased as the months went on. I regularly vomited, passed out, and missed school. I was extremely limited in the amount of time I could spend on school activities, playing sports, and hanging out with friends. My mom took me to my pediatrician, who wasn't sure what was wrong but knew that something wasn't right. She referred me to a gynecologist, who disagreed with the pediatrician's assessment.

"The pain you're feeling is nothing unusual for a girl your age," she said. She prescribed me birth control pills and said I would be fine.

I wasn't.

In eighth grade, when I was fourteen, I returned to that gynecologist. She suspected this time that I might have endo, something I'd never heard of, and she said she'd do surgery to find out. She said the surgery would be laser. I cannot recall if it was electric fulguration or laser ablation, but whichever one it was, she said it was "the best and only option" for me. She did warn my mom and me that I might need another laser surgery down the road because this one would keep the symptoms away for only so long, but she said I should be pain-free for about five years. We didn't know any better, so we agreed to do it.

It was a huge mistake.

She told me after the surgery that I did have endo and that she got as much of it as she could find. I didn't understand that "got" meant "burned" and that there was probably a lot of endo in me that her laser couldn't get. Within a month of the surgery I was in more pain than I had been in before the surgery. I tried to go back to her, but she had moved away. I tolerated the pain as long as I could. That lasted about a year.

I started over with a new gynecologist who, like the first, said that same laser surgery was my best option. We still didn't know any better and figured maybe the first doctor just didn't do it right. So we had her do it and, like after the first, I was in alarming pain a month later. I had no idea how this could be considered the "best option" by two doctors, but what else could I do? I returned to her and she inserted into my uterus an IUD, a form of birth control that reduces the flow during menstruation. It didn't work. In fact, it made me feel a million times worse. When I tried to go back again, I found out that she, too, had moved away.

I was starting to think they were so terrified of my case that they were skipping town. Pretty soon there would be no gynecologists within miles of me.

A year later I went to a third gynecologist who removed the IUD, but she refused to do another surgery.

Why?

She didn't think I needed one.

Why not?

She didn't believe that I was in as much pain as I said I was in. She said she thought the only reason I was complaining of having pain was because I wanted drugs.

Yes! She really said that right to my face!

Oh, but she didn't stop there. She told my mom to consider putting me into an outpatient drug rehabilitation program. My goodness, I had endo, not a drug addiction! Yet this was her professional diagnosis?

I was so angry and confused. How could anyone think that of me? I'd never used drugs. My pain was something I wouldn't wish upon my worst enemy, which was now becoming this doctor. And yet, I was being accused of making it up to get drugs that I didn't want, to fuel an addiction I didn't have. And that was after two surgeries that I was told were the best solutions, only to have each surgery debilitate me more.

After extensive research with my mom over the next year, we found Dr. Seckin, who removed twenty-six lesions with his laparoscopic deep-excision method. Today I am pain-free, and I know that if the endo ever grows back, I have a doctor I can count on.

I don't know why electric fulguration and laser ablation surgeries are allowed to be treatments for endo. Unfortunately, those of us who are in pain who do not know about the disease don't know any better. We just want the pain to go away, and we trust our doctors when they say it's the best option. Believe me when I say you should not get this kind of surgery. Ever. It's incredibly painful. Even if it would have kept me pain-free for the five years that the first doctor said it would, you shouldn't have to have surgery every five years. Take the time to find someone who will do surgery the right way.

CHAPTER 14

From Dependency to Addiction: The Dangers of Pain Medication

Pain medication is not a solution for endometriosis and should not be taken under any circumstances.

When I refer to pain medication, I'm not talking about Advil or Tylenol or something you can buy over the counter. I'm talking about opioids and other highly addictive narcotics that are given to patients today like candy and that ruin lives.

Never will I prescribe you hydrocodone or oxycodone or morphine or fentanyl or any sort of addictive drug, nor should any other doctor. But it happens far too often, and it has been a large contributor to the opioid epidemic in this country, whether other doctors want to admit it or not. I've had twelve-year-old girls come into my office for the first time addicted to a morphine patch. Who in the world gives a girl that young a morphine patch and thinks it's okay? I've had patients in pain beg for narcotics until I'm able to do surgery on them because they've been prescribed them before by other doctors and have been programmed to think that's the answer to their pain. It's not.

Opioids and other addictive narcotics have become dangerous components to endo care because many doctors don't know how else to treat it. It is, to me, an ethical concern. And, sadly, parents sign off on it for their daughters because they trust the doctors and don't want to see their girls in any more pain. These drugs are designed to be effective, but when they wear off, you want more. So, the doctors prescribe more, and more, and more. I don't think doctors who prescribe them understand how they are defacing and eliminating a human being from the surface of the world while the girl is alive.

Amanda, whom you met in the chapter about symptoms, was seventeen when she was told by her doctor to try physical therapy for her pelvic pain. Her doctor prescribed her Valium to relax her muscles. Though Valium is not an opioid—it is considered a sedative and not a pain killer—it is categorized as a highly addictive controlled substance. Every doctor knows that. Yet Amanda was given a bottle of it and told to take it every eight hours as needed.

"I had a full bottle at all times," she said. "It started as being tied to the physical therapy, but since I had plenty of it, it became something I took for the pain at any time, especially when I was away from home at college. My parents even asked the doctor if it was okay for me to do that, and she said it was fine because it was a low dose. I wouldn't say I was addicted to it, but there certainly was a dependency. I felt like there were some things I couldn't do without it. It became a mental dependency, a fear of what might happen if I *didn't* take it."

Amanda was on it for five years. During that time she had not been diagnosed with endo.

"I knew deep down that there was something wrong with me that physical therapy or drugs weren't going to fix," Amanda said. "If I didn't keep speaking up about it, I think the doctor would have kept me on Valium my entire life."

When she found me right after she graduated and I told her that I was confident she had endo, she opted for surgery and ended her dependence on Valium.

"I was entering the working world and knew that the Valium wasn't a good thing to be doing," she said. "I had also just seen a commercial that said nobody should be on Valium for more than two weeks. I thought, 'Well, I'm five years beyond that.' I figured that since I now knew I had endo, there was no reason to continue taking it. I weaned myself off it during the few weeks before my appointment with Dr. Seckin. I had some headaches as a result and was worried about what might happen not being on it, but ultimately it worked out fine. And I knew it was the best thing for me."

Fortunately, Amanda was able to stop without any help. But others, especially those prescribed powerful opioids, aren't as lucky. No matter how much pain you are in, get out of your doctor's office if he or she says you need narcotics. They will not have any direct effect on stopping the endometriosis. And the consequences of the addiction that may develop as a result of taking them could ruin your life and the lives of those who love you.

My Name Is Nicole

"Before long you won't be in control anymore,
even though you'll think that you are."

You're probably expecting a story with a feel-good ending, maybe something about a girl who was prescribed narcotics for endo pain, became addicted, got help, had surgery from Dr. Seckin, and is now pain-free and happier than ever.

Some of that is true, but not all of it.

Twenty-seven years after first being prescribed the opioid narcotic hydrocodone, I'm still on it. I shouldn't be, I don't want to be, and I don't think I will be in a few months, but I'm still working on that.

My first period is about as memorable as a period can be. It came on Christmas Day when I was eleven years old. Nice gift, right? Instead of joyously opening presents, I was rolling on the floor writhing in pain. And it got worse each month that followed. My mom wanted to help, but she didn't know how. My friends didn't understand how something could hurt so much. School administrators couldn't figure out why each month, like clockwork, I'd need to be lifted off the bathroom floor and carried to the office so my mom could take me home. It was frustrating, embarrassing, isolating.

I saw an OB/GYN when I was thirteen; she told me that I might have endo. It was the first time that I'd heard the word, and she didn't say much more about it. She prescribed me a mild pain reliever and sent me home. I had my first laser surgery when I was sixteen after three more years of pain, but it didn't work any better than the pain reliever. That's when my doctor prescribed me hydrocodone. And I was hooked.

I was hooked because it did what a narcotic was supposed to do: provide relief from my pain. I no longer felt like I was dying every day. I was able to attend school and have a social life. I still hurt some, but nothing like before. In a nutshell, I could function, and that was all that mattered to me.

Though I didn't realize it at the time or in the roughly fifteen years that followed, I was addicted. Not in a typical abusive sense. I wasn't stealing pills or living on the streets or taking more than I needed to kill the pain. I went to college and had a professional job. I guess a better word might be that I was "dependent" on the drug. I believed that without it, I wouldn't be able to live my life. And because it was the first "solution" offered to me that actually worked, I didn't think there was any other way. Doctors even coached me on how to use it.

"Take it in advance," they said. "Get ahead of the pain. Don't wait to take it after the pain has already set in."

I followed their advice. If I could have tolerated the pain as I got older, I wouldn't have known it because I never gave it a chance. I recall reading that the major side effect was addiction, but I didn't care. All that mattered was that I was able to work, be with family and friends, and live day to day. The potential consequences didn't matter.

I became more aware of my dependence after I got married. I was thirty-one, and we would have two beautiful children over the next five years. I didn't quit the drug because I never wanted to feel that pain again, but I significantly lessened what I took. During the pregnancies I stayed off it completely, but after each C-section, guess what I was prescribed while my stomach incisions healed? It was becoming obvious why narcotic addiction had become an epidemic.

When my children were born, I knew that I had found my purpose in life. I became a stay-at-home mom who read all the books on child rearing. Everything I did and still do today is dedicated to them. When they were babies I nursed them, read to them, made them homemade baby food, and exposed them to the arts. We go to museums, aquariums, zoos, beaches, and plenty of family gatherings and vacations. I am an active volunteer in their school. While they're in school I focus on my own health so that I have the energy to be the best mom I can be. I work as a yoga instructor. I exercise outside of yoga. I meditate. I pray. I eat well.

And, yes, I still take hydrocodone.

Not because I want to. It doesn't fit the person I've become. When was the last time you heard of an exercising, meditating, spiritual, health-conscious yogi being dependent on narcotics? But it was ingrained in me nearly three decades ago that if I don't take them, the pain would return. And now, with my life so dedicated to my children, I'm especially fearful of that.

This is what narcotics will do to you. Sure, they will mask your physical pain, but they will destroy you mentally. They will make you anxious and mess with your nervous system. They will trap you into thinking that you can't live without them. If you run out of them for even a brief time, they will become your ball-and-chain because you have to have them. Until you're able to get the next supply, they will make you irritable and give you the shakes. And when life happens, such as death, a job loss, or any other negative event, you'll sink into depression, far deeper and darker than if you had been clean. Before long you won't be in control anymore, even though you'll think that you are. The drugs will become a heavy and secret burden in your effort to hide your use from those around you. And to those who know about your dependence, the drugs will become your identity.

I don't consider myself a victim, though I do wonder how things might have been different if I'd been offered something, anything, other than narcotics when I was sixteen. But I've learned it's never too late to change the future. In a few months Dr. Seckin will perform surgery on me. He expects that after surgery, I will never want a narcotic again. I am so excited about the prospect that it is my goal to be completely off them before the surgery.

To every girl reading this, stay far away from narcotics. Don't even start on them, no matter how hard a doctor may try to sell you on them. Don't look at them as something temporary to get you through a tough time, because the chances are pretty good that they will become permanent, even if you don't want them to. There are many other ways to manage your endo pain today, ways that I never knew about when I was young. Don't ever stop looking for that right, healthy solution for you. Tomorrow could always mean something better if you give it a chance.

CHAPTER 15

Avoid Lupron

Lupron is not a narcotic, but it should be avoided like one.

Some doctors will suggest to girls who have significant pain or heavy bleeding during their periods that they should go into menopause. Menopause is when your ovaries stop producing estrogen and progesterone and you no longer have your period. It is a natural part of womanhood that normally begins when you hit your late forties or early fifties.

So how do you go into menopause without aging?

Lupron.

Lupron is a synthetic hormone injected under the skin that sends you into menopause early by suppressing the body's production of estrogen. So even if you are a teenager, Lupron will hormonally trick your body into thinking that you are a middle-aged woman. The idea is that if the estrogen stops, the endo will stop growing and your pain will subside. Being in this "pseudo-menopause" will cause the same effects that a woman who goes through natural menopause feels, such as hot flashes and drastically emotional highs and lows. It's one thing to expect that when you turn fifty, but it's another to experience it when you're much younger.

Many patients have told me that previous doctors prescribed them Lupron, and nearly every single one of them said it was an absolutely horrible experience. They said that sometimes it didn't stop their pain, but even if it did, the side effects were far worse than any pain they'd felt. A simple Google search of Lupron will give you an abundance of articles, websites, and social media groups that are adamantly opposed to this drug.

While the thought of going into menopause to stop endo pain may seem to make some sense, this method is not one I recommend. If you don't want to take that advice from me, read this story from Jenna. Not only was she prescribed Lupron but her doctors attempted to put her on the heavily addictive narcotic Norco, a combination of hydrocodone and the pain reliever acetaminophen.

My Name Is Jenna

"I felt like a guinea pig,
like every doctor was experimenting on me."

Dancing was my life as a young child. I danced nearly every day until about nine years ago, when I turned eleven. That's when my stomach problems started. Instead of dancing, I was regularly curled up on my bedroom floor in pain. I underwent a colonoscopy and an endoscopy, and doctors determined that I had IBS and an intolerance to lactose. I was also told to stay away from gluten and to try a vegan diet. It didn't all necessarily make sense to my mom or me, but I did as they instructed.

When I was thirteen, the summer before my freshman year of high school, and after two years of no improvements, I went to a gynecologist. She did another colonoscopy and endoscopy, both of which she said showed nothing, so she diagnosed me with something completely off the charts: depression. She said that I, a social butterfly with lots of friends, didn't want to go to school. She put me on a strange combination of birth control, Norco, and antidepressants. Fortunately, my mom knew what Norco was and said there was no way she was allowing her thirteen-year-old daughter to take something like that, especially right before the start of school.

Fed up with all of the misdiagnoses, my mom flew me from our home in Texas to California, where we used to live, to see her gynecologist. She trusted him and figured at this stage it was worth a shot. He immediately suspected that I might have endo, and he was correct. He did a quick laser surgery on me and sent me back home. But, as grateful as we were to have a diagnosis and his attempt at treatment, the surgery was a failure. The pain lingered.

I would next go to a pediatric gynecologist at one of Texas's most respected hospitals, where she would perform three laser surgeries over the next year or so and then suggest that I go on a drug called Lupron. My mom didn't know much about Lupron, and the potential side effects scared her when she read them, but when she asked her gynecologist in California for his opinion, he agreed with the Texas doctor that it was fine.

So, at fourteen years old I entered menopause. I took two injections, a one-month dose and a three-month dose, and it was by far the worst experience ever.

Over those four months, the Lupron produced hot flashes, joint pain, an irregular heartbeat, full-body rashes, high blood pressure, constant vomiting, and migraine headaches. I also gained forty pounds over the four months. And the worst part, at least to a fourteen-year-old girl in high school: I lost a lot of hair. When I would wash it in the shower, it would come out in clumps. I hadn't had depression when the gynecologist diagnosed me with it at thirteen, but now I did. I felt like a guinea pig, like every doctor was experimenting on me.

I returned to the pediatric gynecologist and begged her to take me off Lupron. Her response was stunning.

"If you're not going to follow my gold-star standard of treating your endometriosis, I will dismiss you from my practice!"

We never went back to her again.

We found Dr. Seckin when I was sixteen, and I had my first laparoscopic deep-excision surgery. I was pretty young to have surgery like that, but with all of the endo and the scar tissue from the laser surgeries, it needed to be done. I still have some bad cramping at times, but it's nothing I can't handle. Quite honestly, after the Lupron incident, I don't think there's anything that I can't handle.

If someone offers you painkillers or Lupron, I strongly recommend that you don't consider either of them. Who knows, for as much pain as I was in, if I would have become addicted to Norco. And the Lupron? I didn't feel human after it was injected into me.

I know it can be difficult to say no to your doctor, especially if they offer no other alternatives, but you have to muster the courage to say no if you know that what they want to do for you is not the right thing for your body and mind. If you leave their office without a solution for your pain, you will feel lost and defeated. But trust me when I say that that feeling will fade once you get back to work toward finding a doctor who will listen to you and who is educated about this disease. Endo needs to be combated the correct way. Do not settle.

IV

How to Support Her

If you have endometriosis, you cannot confront it
alone. It is vital to have your parents, friends, significant others, teachers, and coaches on your side
as you strive to heal. Here are my thoughts on this
topic spoken directly to those people in your life,
along with some words of wisdom from people
who have served and continue to serve in those
same roles. If you have endo or symptoms of it,
share these stories with those closest to you so that
they can understand how much you need them in
your corner.

CHAPTER 16

To Mothers of Those with Endo

Girls suffering with the symptoms of endometriosis will face a wide range of reactions from their mothers. Some of you will be able to empathize with your daughters because you had the disease. All of you will sympathize, but at what point? For some of you it will be right from the start, but others may take a while to comprehend what she's feeling and the magnitude of it. This could leave your daughter feeling alone and hopeless, which will only compound her grief.

I've found through my thousands of meetings with patients and their mothers that if you're a mother who never went through this, you will more times than not initially side with the notion that menstrual cramps are menstrual cramps. Sure, some girls' cramps may be stronger than others, but how could your daughter's be *that* much worse? Your first, and maybe even second and third reactions, are to give her some ibuprofen and tell her to push through it.

If, when you were your daughter's age, you had pain similar to what she is feeling today but you never received the proper diagnosis or treatment, you are again likely to tell your daughter that it's something she has to work through. You're relaying to her the same message your mother gave you: the pain is normal and part of becoming a woman. Model and television host Padma Lakshmi, a patient of mine with whom I founded the Endometriosis Foundation of America, experienced that reaction from her mother.

"I got my period when I was thirteen years old," Padma said. "And probably from the first or second month that I had my period, I was bedridden for at least two to three days a month. I had extreme pain in my pelvic area, in my back, in my head, but most of all in my heart. My mother, who was a nurse and a very educated women, told me that she suffered from many of the same symptoms and that some girls got it, and some girls didn't. This was my lot in life. I believed her because my mother is a very sincere person."

And then there are some of you, whether you had endo yourself or not, who truly believe right from the start that something is out of order inside your daughter's body, and you will do everything you can for her. But oftentimes, despite how hard you try or how many doctors you take her to, nothing seems to work. You don't give up on her, but you quietly mourn with feelings of guilt and helplessness.

I am not a psychologist, though I certainly see and address the emotions patients and their mothers encounter. What I've learned over the past three-plus decades is that the best thing you can do for your daughter, above all else, is believe her.

When you believe her unconditionally, no matter how many times she is denied by doctors, other family members, or friends, you and your daughter will stay on the path toward healing. It may be a long and arduous path with many obstacles, but when you stick by her side, the two of you will eventually get there together. Without that love and care from you, a thick layer of mental anguish will be added to your daughter's physical pain, and that can be insurmountable for her to overcome alone.

Donna, the mother of one of my patients, has compelling insight about this, which may help you get into the frame of mind that your daughter needs you to be in right now.

My Name Is Donna

*"Don't ever doubt your daughter and
the pain she says she is in."*

You read in the first section the story written by my daughter, Stephanie. Her symptoms first flared when she was twelve years old in middle school, and they continued nonstop through college and beyond. The first doctor she ever saw for the symptoms misdiagnosed her with IBS. Another twelve doctors and a decade later, still with no diagnosis of endo, she was told once again that she probably had IBS. Her story had gone full circle, and I walked that circle with her every step of the way.

I think I speak for all mothers when I say that there is nothing more heartbreaking than watching our children suffer, and there is nothing more frustrating than not knowing how to make things better for them. We moms are natural nurturers, darn good at what we do, and it's very rare when we don't know how to lessen or eliminate our children's physical or emotional pain. But endometriosis is unlike most diseases. It's so sneaky, so powerful, and so unknown to the masses, including doctors. It's a horrific combination that can and does fool the best moms.

I'd heard of endometriosis before Stephanie had started feeling pain, but like most people, I knew little about it and didn't have the knowledge to tie it to any of her symptoms. Our family had no history of it, and I never knew any friends who had it. When we took Stephanie to that first doctor, I had no reason not to believe him that IBS was the source of her pain. I didn't know much about the disorder, but simply put, he was the expert, and I wasn't. Plus, based on what he told us, the symptoms seemed to match. I left his office that day feeling good, that we were getting to the bottom of her pain. I would do everything I could to help Stephanie get back to being a normal teenager.

Things got tricky, though, when it became obvious after some time that what Stephanie had went well beyond IBS. With more symptoms emerging, we went to another doctor to get a second opinion. After some tests, doctors determined that she had a gluten allergy. So, she gave up gluten. When the symptoms persisted, we went back again, and after more tests, we were told that she had an allergy to lactose. So, we cut lactose from her diet. While these allergy diagnoses were accurate, we were led to believe that they were the causes of her symptoms, but they weren't. As a mother, I'd never been through something like this. I'd always had the ability to make my daughter better. But in this case, though I'd invested an immense amount of time and effort, she seemed to be getting worse by the day.

Something to understand from an emotional perspective is that each diagnosis Stephanie received was more than a diagnosis to us; it was hope. She'd been through so much, and we both wanted nothing more than for her to heal, so each new diagnosis from a new doctor led us to believe that we were a step closer to the finish line. But then another symptom, such as bladder issues, would arise. And then another symptom, like bloating, would occur. They were coming at her with such ferocity. A new diagnosis would raise our spirits, but then another symptom would sink us even lower.

Watching her go through this was agonizing beyond anything I'd ever experienced. I wanted to trade places with her, as every mother would. I felt helpless at times. Never hopeless, because I certainly wasn't going to give up on her, but when doctor after doctor can't tell you what's wrong or leads you to believe that it's something it's not, you begin to wonder where to turn next or from where that next bit of hope will come.

Endo attacks every girl differently, and the dynamics of each girl and family and support system are diverse, so I cannot give you specific advice pertinent to your daughter. What I can offer you, though, are a few general ideas of the effort that you as a mother can make to get her through this. It's an effort that I believe is essential to her conquering this disease and coming out the other side a new and vibrant person.

First, and most important, don't ever doubt your daughter and the pain she says she is in. You may think, "Of course I would never doubt my daughter!" And I didn't doubt Stephanie. But I know there are many wonderful and loving moms who have, because that's the power endo has. Nobody is to blame for those feelings; it's the nature of the beast. Endo messes with the body and psyche of the person it's directly attacking, it muddles the minds of those who are trying to help that person, and it wears down all parties involved to the point that you question everything that's happening. Seriously, how could we have been to thirteen doctors in more than a decade and not have known what was wrong with Stephanie? I learned that it's not only possible but it's probable when endo is the root cause.

Take your daughter's side, no matter how much you've been through or how exhausted it makes you. She's been through far more, and she needs you to fight for her. If your daughter loses you as her advocate, she may lose any hope she has left.

Second, continually seek resolutions for your daughter, regardless of how sure a doctor may seem about a diagnosis. Don't ever trust that your doctor knows everything, and don't ever stop asking him or her (or yourself) questions. I used to believe that when I walked into a doctor's office with my daughter, what they said about her health was gold. But I learned, especially with this disease, that's not always the case. A lot of doctors aren't educated about endo. I believe that will change one day; it already is changing with the awareness that's been created in just the last few years. But there is a long way to go.

The one regret I have in how I pursued this with Stephanie is that I didn't press the gynecologist who first suggested the possibility that she could have endo. I didn't question her, because she immediately followed that with, "But I doubt that's what you have." As soon as she opened that door to the possibility, I should have pounced on it. But I believed her because she was the professional, so we moved on. Fortunately, Stephanie never forgot that the gynecologist had said that. As Stephanie said in her story, the seed had been planted. It just took a while for either of us to do anything about it.

Third, don't stop searching until you find a medical professional who truly understands what endo is. It must be someone with a solid reputation, who believes your daughter when she describes her pain, who has the expertise a specialist should have, who has a bedside manner that someone in her condition deserves, and who has a remedy that makes sense. I've heard about women with endo who see specialists, but they find out those "specialists" know less about endo than they do. That's where your knowledge about the disease and ability to ask thoughtful questions will help immensely, which is exactly why Stephanie and I and others are sharing our stories with you.

Take this book and other literature with you wherever you go and state your case. Demand that you be heard. After Stephanie's second IBS diagnosis from the thirteenth doctor, after she cried all the way home from that appointment, we got on the internet and found Dr. Seckin. Our guts told us he was the one to see. And if we had felt after meeting with him that he wasn't the answer, we'd have continued our pursuit immediately until we found the right person.

I had one goal for Stephanie since the first symptoms kicked in when she was twelve, and that was for her to be well as soon as humanly possible. It took far longer than I had wanted or expected because I didn't know what disease she had or the scope of it. But if you stay by your daughter's side, keep asking questions, and find that one person who knows how to help you the right way, you will reach that goal. Don't stop fighting for your daughter.

CHAPTER 17

To Fathers of
Those with Endo

Men don't have periods. For that obvious reason alone, you as a father ordinarily aren't involved in your daughter's menstrual cycle. If she's having her first period, it's likely her mother will show her what to do. If she needs some supplies, her mother will buy them. If she's displaying new emotions because of her periods, her mother will talk to her. If she's feeling pain, again, her mother. Most boys and even men are surprised when they find out that the female body goes through monthly bleeding. And if they do know, they don't have any concept of what abnormal bleeding is.

It makes perfect sense that Mom would be the go-to person, because Mom is a woman who understands a period far better than you do. But dads and all men, in my opinion, should know more about a woman's menstrual cycle than they do. The more you can understand about any difficulty that someone goes through, the more capacity and desire you will have to help. That's why, as I discussed in the first section, boys should be taught about the female anatomy at a young age. They should understand not just the science behind the female body, but the emotional, psychological, and sociological realties of being a woman.

For you fathers who see your daughters in pain and don't know what to do, the suggestions would be the same that Donna and I gave to mothers: believe your daughter, search for answers to her pain, and find an expert who can help fix it and provide your daughter hope. But here's one additional piece of advice: do not distance your-self from the situation. It's one thing for her mother to step up for the typical menstrual cycle issues. It's another for you to expect her mother to provide all of the assistance your daughter requires when endo is involved. Your daughter needs both of you. Her symptoms should not scare you away or make you convince yourself that she'd be better off with just her mother. Be there for her.

My Name Is Richard

"We must always be prepared to defend them,
even in uncomfortable situations."

My daughter, Rachel, spoke to you about her decade-long battle with endometriosis. She was the one who had dressed up as a
football player with her girlfriends for Halloween, but she couldn't
be in the pictures they took at school because she was slumped in
the hallway corner in pain. She had been told repeatedly by several
people that what she felt was normal. She was misdiagnosed by
doctor after doctor, not a single one able to determine her ailment.
One gynecologist told her to take six Advil at a time. Another one
tried to push the narcotic Percocet on her. Rachel cried tears of joy
after her successful surgery with Dr. Seckin, because she had never
thought the day would come that she would be well again.

When Rachel first felt pain during her period in high school,
her mother handled it 100 percent of the time. I was aware that
something was going on, but that was it. Dads are not normally
involved in that aspect of our daughters' lives. We don't have periods, we don't know much of the terminology used with regard to a
menstrual cycle, and we certainly are not qualified to give suggestions of how to manage pain from it. I can't imagine what I would
have said to Rachel if she'd walked up to me as a teenager and said,
"Dad, I'm having my period and it really, really hurts. What can I
do?" I was never in the discussion, which I was perfectly fine with
and I would bet Rachel was fine with, too. I'm not even sure, if I'd
had more knowledge and had offered suggestions, if she would have
felt comfortable taking advice from her dad.

My attitude completely changed when Rachel went from one doctor to another with no success. Some of them misdiagnosed her. Some didn't diagnose her at all. They offered solutions that didn't make sense. Six Advil at once? Whatever was happening to her was affecting every piece of her life, from school to work to her social life, and it was something beyond any knowledge my wife or I had. As her father, watching her go through this day after day broke my heart to pieces.

During this journey there were some rare times, admittedly, when I wondered if her pain was as dreadful as she had claimed. Not because I didn't believe my daughter, but because I couldn't figure out how all the doctors we were trusting with her care couldn't come up with a single accurate diagnosis or treatment. I couldn't understand how I'd never heard of any other women with this, not knowing at the time how silent this disease was. I knew Rachel was telling the truth, but how come we couldn't piece together this puzzle after so many attempts?

When Dr. Seckin came out of surgery and told my wife and me how much endo he'd found inside her, I could see how distraught he was that no doctor prior could help her. We were upset and relieved all at once. Upset at the doctors who dismissed her and upset at ourselves for not knowing about this disease, yet relieved that this nightmare was coming to an end. When we got home after her surgery, I logged into my computer and read all I could about endo. Everything I had found fit Rachel's profile—the pain, the misdiagnoses, the lack of public awareness. It was information and knowledge I wished I'd had ten years earlier.

I realize today that there wasn't a whole lot more we could have done for Rachel. We are proactive parents. We took Rachel to the doctor as soon as she had felt pain, and we continued going from doctor to doctor. I can't say that I wish we'd have done more in that respect. If there are any regrets that I have, they are that I didn't know about this disease, and that I didn't know much about a woman's menstrual cycle in general.

If you would have tried to tell me when I was fifteen years old that I should know more about how a girl's body works, I would have laughed at you. But if you told me that today, as a father who went through this with Rachel, I would completely agree with you. Men need to be educated about this kind of stuff, and preferably at a young age so that it isn't so taboo when they get older. As fathers, we need to know what's going on in our daughters' teenage bodies so that we can genuinely help them when they need it. If we don't know about their bodies, it's almost impossible to know about endo. Given the power and scope of this disease, that attitude has to change.

I still don't know all there is to know about a woman's period and cycle, and I probably never will. And I think that's okay. But I learned that I needed to know more than I did, and now I do. I know enough to help Rachel if this chronic disease ever returns, or to help any young girl in my family or circle of friends who has such pain. We as fathers will all say that we will defend our daughters to the death, but if we are serious about that, we must always be prepared to defend them, even in uncomfortable situations or ones that require us to learn something that we were ignorantly told at a young age we'd never need to know.

Take the time to learn about women's health and endometriosis. The more you know, the more equipped you'll be to stand up for your daughter.

CHAPTER 18

To Girls with Endo and Their Significant Others

You may feel uncomfortable explaining endometriosis to your significant other. You may feel self-conscious talking about it because there is a chance you could be misunderstood or rejected by your partner. As a result, you may choose to try to suffer in silence.

Even dating at a young age can be problematic because of endo symptoms. If you cannot stand on your feet because of the pain or if you're bleeding heavily all night, how do you conceal your pain while also remaining in the present moment with your partner?

Bankes, who talked to you about empowerment, hasn't done much dating lately because of the disease.

"I had my first high school boyfriend three years ago," she said. "Since then I haven't dated anyone. Endo is so personal. Trying to explain it to a teenage boy is crazy. They're like, 'What? So if you don't have your period now, then you're okay, right?' They can't comprehend it."

If you have endo or the symptoms of it, it's up to you whether or not you want to tell your new romantic partner about it. But if you hope the relationship is going to work long-term, you will have to tell them at some point, and I would suggest sooner rather than later. If they can't back you up, then, in my opinion, they're likely not worth keeping around. This disease consumes you until you can get it properly treated, and because it is chronic, it will likely be part of you in some way after it's treated. That means it will have to be part of your partner's life if your relationship is going to work.

Mel was eighteen when she started dating Chris. She wasn't diagnosed with endo until she was twenty, and two years later she and Chris were married. I'll let them tell you their story together.

Our Names Are Mel and Chris

*"If you really love her,
you will do everything you can to help her."*

Mel: I knew when I got my first period at fourteen that it was worse than it should have been. I would get so sick that I would pass out. I talked to my mom about it, but she really didn't know what to do. She assumed that it was something I had to deal with on my own. I wouldn't see a gynecologist for the first time until I was eighteen. When I did go, the gynecologist said, "Well, that's not normal." He brought up the word "endometriosis," but he said he didn't think I had it. He put me on birth control, and that was it.

It was also right around that time that Chris and I had started dating. We were open and honest about everything in our relationship from the start, so I didn't hesitate to tell him about it. When I did, I was confident that he would fully support me and do all that he could to help me.

Chris: She told me she'd had symptoms for years, like abnormal pain and bad periods. While I couldn't say that I knew much about that, I was glad she shared it with me. She was in pain almost every day we were together, and I hated seeing it. As soon as she told me, I was just as determined as she was to find the source of it and get her better.

Mel: Two years later when I was twenty, with the pain still there, my gynecologist did an ultrasound and said, "Yeah, you may have endo." He said he could do ablation surgery on me. I was really terrified and confused because, no joke, I spotted in the corner of his office a book called, *Endometriosis for Dummies*. I left there in tears. I was going to be opened up for laser surgery by a "dummy"? When I got home I looked up endo online, but I couldn't find much on it. It felt defeating. So, I went ahead with the surgery because I didn't know what else to do. When it was finished, the doctor told me I was in stage I or II.

A short time later my pain was back, and it was worse than before the surgery. I went to a different doctor, one at a prestigious hospital in my hometown who worked in the endo wing of the building, and she said the pain I felt throughout my body couldn't be endo.

"Honey," she said, "endo can only grow in the uterus. It can't grow anywhere else."

That's what I was told in the twenty-first century by a female doctor whose specialty was endometriosis.

I left her office angry, and I started looking again. That's when I found Dr. Seckin's first book and read the stories of the women who had endo. I cried. I knew this was what I had, and I knew that I had to see him. He was six hundred miles away, but I told my mom and Chris, who was now my fiancé, that I was going to New York. I went into surgery with Dr. Seckin thinking that I'd come out fifty percent better, and that would have been awesome, but I came out feeling ninety-five percent better.

Chris: When Dr. Seckin told us she had endo and that the laser surgery had done more damage than good, I was sad, but I was also relieved to finally know what was going on. All of those trips to clinics and doctors and the ER, and nobody could make Mel better. At some of those visits we'd been told that there wasn't much known about endo and that there was really no easy way to help her. Obviously, those people were wrong.

Mel: From the day we started dating, Chris would go to appointments with me and be involved however he could. He'd take care of me after surgeries and be there every step of the way. We've been married a little over a year now. The most difficult part of our relationship when we didn't know what was wrong was the painful sex. We didn't feel much like newlyweds. We knew if we had sex that I would be in so much pain during and after that we didn't really know if it was worth it.

Chris: It did take a toll on our sex life. We had an undisclosed mutual agreement that we wouldn't do it that often because she would be in so much pain. She would literally be in tears when we would try, and it would make me feel terrible. I would be the one to say no when she would want to try, because I didn't want to see her hurting like that. I just tried to support her as much as I could. I knew it wasn't her fault. This was the luck of the draw her body got.

Mel: I couldn't imagine going through this without him. I have been so blessed to have him by my side. From the day I first told him about my symptoms he has been there for me.

Chris: To anyone out there whose partner is going through this disease, understand that they are not to blame. They did not ask for this. Yes, it will cause stress in your relationship at times, but if you really love her, you will do everything you can to help her.

CHAPTER 19

To Girls with Endo and Their Friends

Our true friends are the ones who stand by us unconditionally and without judgment during our most trying times, and they listen without preaching. Nearly every patient of mine, past and present, has a story about losing friends because of endo. If a friend believes you when you say you are sick—and you would expect that she would since she's your friend—why would she be upset because you can't go out as much as she'd like you to? Why would she get angry because you are in pain all the time? Shouldn't a friend act the opposite way and do what she can to try to get you through it? But, like so many others, she questions your claims because she doesn't understand what you're going through. And you can't explain it because you don't know yourself what's going on with your body. Rather than try her best to understand it and be there for you, she finds it easier to sever ties.

You met Amanda, who shared her story about being prescribed all of the Valium that she wanted. As the pain became more severe, she struggled socially.

"When I was in college and got sick, I had this group of girls who were close friends, but they totally ditched me," Amanda said. "They said, 'You're a dud,' and 'You're sick all the time,' and 'If you were really sick you'd have proof.' They cut me out of chat groups and did things without me, and these were twenty-one-year-old women! The worst part was my best friend among the bunch was the leader of it all. They turned out to be the rudest girls I'd ever met."

Amanda said she figured out who her true friends were and stuck with them.

"For all these young girls in middle school and high school who have these symptoms, you need to find the girls who will be there for you," she said. "Once I got to college and met those girls who would eventually turn on me, most who were in my sorority, I was kind of alone with my pain. Find the right support system and stay away from the others."

Amanda said the "best friend" who was the leader in the uprising against her has since tried to reach out to her.

"She knows that I had a successful surgery and that I'm doing better. I think that opened her eyes a little and she felt bad about how she treated me," Amanda said. "She tried to message me about a book that said people who had endo used to be told that they had hysteria. She said, 'That was you!' But I didn't respond. People's true colors will show when you are going through a challenging time. They need to be there for you *all* the time, not just when it's convenient. I've found that ones I have known since middle school and high school, along with a few wonderful college friends, are the ones who keep in touch with me today and ask me how I'm doing. You need to treasure people like that."

Take Amanda's advice. Anyone who does not stand by your side when you are going through endo symptoms is probably not worth hanging on to as a friend. As you'll read in the next story, find the Amy in your life.

Our Names Are Meg and Amy

"The few times that I did find myself about to judge her . . .
I checked myself right there."

Meg: I was in fifth grade when I started having pain, a few years before I would get my first period. It was not uncommon for me to be doubled over, unable to walk. It carried over to middle school and high school, where I would miss weeks of school at a time. When I would complain to the nurse about my cramps, she'd give me a heating pad and tell me to lay down. She never wanted me to leave school early, but I usually had to because I couldn't pay attention in class.

I saw about every doctor possible as a teenager: a gynecologist, who put me on birth control; a gastroenterologist, who couldn't figure out the source of pain; a rheumatologist, who also had no idea; a neurologist, who diagnosed me with anxiety; and an ER doctor who said I had appendicitis. He opened me up and determined my appendix was fine, but he removed it anyway.

I went to college, still with no diagnosis and no solutions. I bled for a month straight and went to the hospital, where I was told that bleeding for a month wasn't abnormal. I finally had to go home because I was getting nothing accomplished at school. I went to my gynecologist, who said he'd do surgery to see what he could find. When I woke up he said that he had found nothing and that he was certain the pain was all in my mind.

I returned to school later my freshman year and for most of my sophomore year before finally dropping out the summer before my junior year. I couldn't do it anymore. Thinking about it now, I'm not sure how I made it as long as I did. Well, actually, yeah I do know. It was my friend, Amy.

Amy: Meg and I met in the first couple of days of our freshman year, and we hit it off right away. She had to leave a few weeks into the semester because she was having surgery to see what was going on with her body. I knew she was constantly in pain, but I didn't know why. I knew that even she didn't know what was going on.

When she came back for the second semester, my roommate had left, so Meg and I became roommates and better friends. We had a typical college friendship, going out to concerts and to eat and doing fun things, but it was hard for her. She was always tired and in pain. She would explain how distressing it was and wondered if it was all in her head. As her friend, it was so tough for me because neither of us knew what was going on. I felt helpless. I didn't want to use a cliché and say, "Oh, it'll get better," because I really didn't know if that was true.

Her symptoms were worse when we started sophomore year. She couldn't sleep at night, and she'd pass out from exhaustion after her classes. Yet, she never gave up. She knew from the beginning that she wanted to go to medical school, so she did internships and whatever else she could to make herself better in school. It was really inspiring to watch her.

Meg: From middle school through college, I definitely lost friendships. I was on the dance teams in middle school and high school, but I missed a lot of practices and had to sit out of performances. Friends would ask what was wrong, and I'd blame it on my asthma because I didn't want to talk about my period. I knew they wouldn't understand anyway. All that concerned them was that I couldn't do anything fun. It's hard to grow close to people, especially when you're young, when you can't do things with them.

But that's how Amy was different.

She and I talked all the time, even when I had to leave college for extended periods, and she didn't hesitate to be my roommate despite what I was going through. When I couldn't get out of bed, she'd get food for me. She says I was an inspiration to her for not giving up, but it was Amy who pushed me to not give up trying to figure out what my body was doing. I know none of this was easy for her, but I guess that's what true friendship is. She was there to listen to me. She was the one I would go to when I knew I couldn't count on anyone else. She never tried to tell me that I was being dramatic. Even when I told her I wasn't returning to school for junior year, she understood. After I left school, when I was finally diagnosed by Dr. Seckin and had surgery, Amy was there for me.

Amy: I know she lost friends who were cruel to her. They'd ask, "Why doesn't she just push through?" or say, "I think it's all in her head." And I'll admit, it wasn't always easy for me, especially when neither of us had answers. But she never gave up on us, either. What I mean is that I think she pushed herself to do the fun things we were able to do together because, no matter how much it hurt, she wanted to be a good friend to me. She sacrificed a lot.

The few times that I did find myself about to judge her, because I didn't understand her condition or wondered how much of it was real, I checked myself right there. And that's the difference between being a good friend and not. I realized this was out of her control. When you see that pain and despair, you have to realize that this is so much more than her having a bad period. Her friends at the time, who were also my friends, didn't get it because they didn't see it like I did.

There was no real secret formula to what I did. I didn't try to offer her advice. I just listened a lot and validated her experiences.

Instead of saying, "You'll be fine," I'd say, "That really sucks." I also didn't tell her how strong she was because I didn't want to pressure her into thinking that's how she had to be. I told her it was okay to take a break from school, to take care of herself, and to let her body rest. We all put ourselves on this rigid timeline, that we're supposed to graduate at a certain time and get a professional job at a certain time. I let her know that she didn't have to do that, and I think that helped her a lot. We're like soul sisters. We speak the same language and really care about each other.

Meg: I'm still coming to terms with the fact that I have endo because I was told for so long that I didn't have it, but I'm progressing. I work in a doctor's office part time and will be back to school in the fall. I want to be a doctor one day. I used to want to be one because of the asthma I've had since I was a kid, but now I have a huge interest in gynecology. I want to assist other women who have endo. I want to be that one who listens to them and believes them, the way Dr. Seckin and my best friend, Amy, listened to and believed me.

CHAPTER 20

To Girls with Endo and Their Teachers

Our education system in the United States is underfunded. Classrooms are overcrowded. Teachers pay for classroom supplies out of their own pockets. Demands on them, from keeping kids physically safe to prepping them for standardized tests, are overwhelming. Yet I have to ask these teachers to add more to your plate, because one in ten girls of childbearing age has or will have endometriosis. It will affect their ability to perform in school, participate in activities, and simply attend class, which will have an overall negative effect on their lives into adulthood.

Nearly everyone who has shared a story about endo in this book or anywhere else had her school career affected by the disease. Because when the pain is that horrid and that frequent, it will undoubtedly affect what she's supposed to be doing five days a week for nine months a year until she's at least eighteen.

"I had to be homeschooled most of the year that I had all those surgeries," Lynn said. Lynn shared her story with you about the three unsuccessful laser surgeries she'd had over the course of ten months. "I went for about a quarter of my junior year, but then I had to be homeschooled because I was in so much pain. I was fortunate when I was in school, though, that the teachers and staff gave me a lot of encouragement and understood the condition I was in."

Unfortunately, many teachers and staff members don't understand because they may not know what the disease is, which is no different from much of the general public. But it's so important that you do understand, just as you try to understand other barriers your students face. Kids underperform in school for many reasons beyond their control. Having endometriosis, a disease that cripples young girls daily, could be another real reason why they struggle.

Through my foundation, we are working in schools year-round to spread the word about endo. Our ENPOWR program (Endometriosis: Promoting Outreach and Wide Recognition) has taught more than one thousand lessons on endometriosis in over two hundred schools to thirty-five thousand students. Our goal is to one day be in every school in every state so that all girls can catch this disease early with as little impact on their education as possible. The program, which can be in your school with just a phone call or an email to endofound.org, can be taught by you or by one our volunteers.

But, aside from the program, I want all teachers to know that if a student tells you she cannot get her work done or needs to run to the bathroom multiple times a day because she has this thing called endometriosis, it's serious. How you address it in your classroom is for you to decide, but please understand how dire her situation is, both physically and mentally. She needs as much support as she can get, including from the people in the place where she spends most of her days.

My Name Is Liz

"My class became a safe place that gave her
the power to speak freely about endo."

I'm a biology teacher at an International Baccalaureate college prep school. One of my students was Bankes, who spoke to you about empowerment. We're a four-year high school, but our curriculum is so rigorous that the courses our students take beginning their freshman year are college-level.

Given my science background and what I teach, I've known for years what endometriosis is. I also have several girlfriends who have had the disease. But I would bet many teachers around the world, including some biology teachers, probably fall into the same category as most everyone else when it comes to endo: they've never heard of it. And while not all teachers need to know it to do their jobs, I think it's important that they are at least aware of the disease and how devastating it can be. Why? Based on statistics, they likely have students who have it, and those students need their teachers' and schools' support as they try to manage their endo while keeping up with their classes.

Bankes explained to you that her symptoms started when she was twelve and flared up on holidays and vacations, including during a trip to Italy. Last year, her senior year, she missed several days of school and a lot of the special senior activities. After she was finally able to get the surgery she needed, she returned to school and asked me if she could share with the class details about her disease and all it had put her through. I agreed to let her.

Of course, since this was biology, the setting was conducive for such a discussion; I wouldn't expect this to take place during third-period calculus. But my point is that as her teacher, I gave her the time and space and platform to tell her story, as I would hope that a teacher in every school would do for a student in her position, if asked. I wanted the other students and myself to understand what she'd been going through, why she'd missed so much school, and why she couldn't participate in many senior events. Bankes was able to share with us not just the biology and anatomy of her journey but the emotions behind it. She gave us a look into the hidden side—the pain she carried each day. My classroom became a safe place that gave her the power to speak freely about endo. She went from being that kid some may have narrowly viewed as regularly being sick and out from school, to being someone they now understood, someone with whom they could sympathize and even empathize.

Bankes had done an incredible job of hiding her disease from teachers and other students. I can't imagine how many days she was in school and in agony, yet none of us noticed. And when she was absent, she kept up with her work. Given the high-level classes and that she graduated on time, it shows how determined she was to not let this disease become her identity. I'm sure it was difficult for her to try to communicate and justify to some teachers and administrators why she was out so much while also trying to hide what she was experiencing, especially when teachers know that a "disease" called "senioritis" kicks in for some seniors each year, but she successfully did what she had to do.

We as teachers have demanding jobs. We have students from all backgrounds to teach, students who learn in different ways, students who have things going on in their lives outside of school that would shock us if we knew. For those reasons, my message is not just to teachers of students with endo but to the student with endo herself.

Pain is universal, but it is also subjective and cannot always be quantified. We all have pain in some way, be it physical or emotional, but it may not be easy to convey to others how strong and deep that pain is. Sometimes teachers will want to "see" the pain to know that their student isn't trying to get out of an assignment or class, or that the student has a legitimate reason for not doing homework or needing more time to complete a project. If you break your arm, yes, every teacher is going to have some idea of the pain you are feeling and the obstacles ahead of you until it has healed. But if you tell a teacher, "I'm having an excessively painful period," especially a male teacher, that person may show no sympathy or empathy because they don't understand the source of your pain or how awful it is.

I would recommend explaining the disease to your teachers the best you can, providing them with literature they can read. And give them a scale of how bad the pain is. "On a scale of one to ten, it's a nine." Or, "It's probably similar to the pain you feel when giving birth, but worse, and it lasts longer." Every woman who has naturally given birth, and men who have been in the delivery room to witness such births, should be able to comprehend that.

From Bankes's stories and from seeing my friends with endo go through it, I know how chronic and painful the disease is. But most teachers won't know. If you're a student with endo, explain it to your teachers in the simplest terms possible so that they can appreciate your misery. And if you're a teacher who is approached by a student who says she has endo, understand how real and gruesome the disease is. She isn't making it up, and she isn't exaggerating. Imagine trying to teach your class daily with pain shooting relentlessly through your abdomen or down your leg, with your bowels attacking you, with fatigue so strong that you can't stand up. It would be impossible. The cards are stacked against any girl with endo. She could really use you on her side to help her fight through it, even if it means just under-standing the reasons behind her absences and accommodating her the best you can.

CHAPTER 21

To Girls with Endo and Their Coaches

Coaching is much like teaching. You are trying to provide the youth on your team with the knowledge and skills they will need to excel. You train them and encourage them to give their best effort. When they don't perform well, you keep working with them to improve. When they shine, you push them a little harder.

And when they are injured?

You may continue working with the other players, but you don't give up on that injured person. As frustrating as it may be not having them there to participate, you don't blame them for the setback that their body has inflicted upon them.

At least you shouldn't.

What I want coaches to understand about endo is the same thing that I want teachers, parents, significant others, and everyone else to understand, and it's the same thing Chris said about his wife, Mel: it's not her fault.

Dilara told you that she had a female swim coach who yelled at her for being in so much pain and told her to "just swim," even though Dilara couldn't move. If Dilara had entered her swim practice on crutches with a cast on her leg that she broke in a car accident the day before, would the coach have yelled at her to "just swim"? No. Just because you cannot see the pain or injury doesn't mean it's not there. If one of your athletes tries to explain to you that she has endometriosis, or if she doesn't know what she has but is describing the symptoms of the disease to you, please listen to her and do your best to show some compassion. When athletes sprain ankles or breaks bones or tear ACLs, coaches are completely sympathetic because they know what those injuries are and how painful they can be. Well, believe me when I say that if one of your athletes tells you she has endo, she would trade it for a sprained ankle, broken bone, or torn ACL in a heartbeat.

The next story, told by Sophie and her track coach, Prince, is an example of the ideal coach and student relationship.

Our Names Are Sophie and Prince

"Prince didn't fully understand what was going on with my body, but he never doubted me."

Sophie: I was diagnosed with endometriosis when I was a freshman in high school, about four years after my first very painful period. My doctor put me on birth control to ease the pain, but it didn't help, so he did laser surgery on me after my freshman year. I felt fine for a few months, until a cyst materialized and burst. The physical pain was punishing, but it was worse mentally. I thought we had fixed my problems, and now I was back to where I started. Pediatric endometriosis was outside of my doctor's expertise, and when my symptoms and pain persisted, he stopped responding to my calls and would not see me. I eventually found Dr. Seckin, who did a successful surgery on me prior to my senior year.

One of the hardest parts of having endo in high school was that I ran track. I wasn't great at it, but I gave it my all and really enjoyed it. After my surgery and before the season started, I explained my condition to Prince (he insisted we call him by his first name "Prince" and not "coach"). He was a very tough but approachable coach, and he insisted that we always be honest with him. I think I may have been a little too honest when I explained what endo was—he had that "too much information" expression on his face—but he listened and understood.

Prince: Endometriosis was news to me when Sophie brought it to me, and yeah, I was probably giving her weird looks. But I've told every kid I've ever coached that if they need to have a conversation with me, they need to spit it out and talk to me. I'm not a dictator, and I'm never going to throw them under a bus. Yeah, I'm probably the toughest coach they will ever have. But if they can't feel comfortable enough to talk to me, then that's when I need to question myself as a coach, because eventually it's going to negatively affect their performance. If we can move forward and go someplace together as coach and athlete, then I'm happy. Sophie is in college now, and she's saying I had an impact on her. To that, I say "bingo!" I did my job.

Sophie: As discouraging as my situation was, I didn't quit. If I wasn't feeling well, I showed up to practice if I could, and I think he appreciated that. I never missed any meets, whether I was competing or not.

At one point during my sophomore year, I kind of took over as a team manager when I couldn't run. That didn't go over well with some of my teammates, who didn't like one of their peers telling them what to do during drills. One time, when Prince noticed a boy and a couple of girls giving me a hard time about it, he pulled them aside and questioned them about their behavior, ordering them to stop. He had my back, just as he did with all of his athletes.

Prince: Sophie was there at practice trying to help and learn. I usually have my younger kids try to learn some things from my older kids. This was a case of her being pretty young and telling the older kids what to do. But I told them that I gave her instructions to do it, and no matter what the reason, they could choose to listen to her or go home. Once I said that, they were fine. Everybody means something on my team, even if they can't do what the other kids can do.

Sophie: I'm grateful for how nice Prince was to me throughout high school. People always asked me why I was in so much pain and why I was missing a lot of school. Some girls would tell me to take a couple of Advil and get over it. Prince didn't fully understand what was going on with my body, but he never doubted me. He also made me comfortable by not acting like it was unusual, and that's a good lesson for everybody. Though endo may be new to you, it really helps, if I tell you about it, for you to not respond with something like, "I don't know how you can live with that." It's nice that people try to empathize, but it also makes me feel different. Like Prince did, just listen and tell me you'll support me however you can. That's what I need to hear.

Prince: You have to treat everybody as an individual. As a coach I'm forced to sit in some of these workshops administrators make you attend about how to sympathize and empathize, and I'm thinking to myself, "Why am I here? Just treat the kids like human beings." The way I see it, we are here to change lives in a positive way. Yes, I'll put you through some stuff training-wise that you've never been through, but in the long run it's going to be beneficial to your mind and body. They need to learn about things in life that you can't get from a book. I believe the best lessons are taught and learned by having conversations with people. Sophie had a lot of issues. A lot. It wasn't my goal to get myself through it. It was my goal to find a way to keep her involved and make her better, even when she couldn't run. In the end, I think our conversations and relationship made both of us better.

EPILOGUE

Endurance

I stated in the introduction that I wanted this book to "fully arm you with the truth and knowledge about the disease so that you can overcome your fears and confidently stand up for yourself." I hope that the women who have heroically shared their stories have achieved that goal.

There are many similarities and differences in these women's stories, from their symptoms, misdiagnoses, the ages at which they started feeling pain, the number of years it took to be properly diagnosed, to the reactions from their family and friends, and the effects the disease had on their schoolwork and social lives.

But the one quality that each story shared, the same quality that they share with every single one of my patients I've cared for during my career, is that they never stopped.

They never stopped listening to their bodies.

They never stopped searching for answers to their symptoms.

They never stopped questioning those who failed to help them.

They never stopped believing that they deserved better.

They never stopped trusting that someone would eventually come through for them.

Yes, they had doubts along the way. They had their hopes shaken at times. But they rose up and kept going. They kept pursuing. They kept pushing. They kept demanding. Their persistence is why they are healed or on a path toward healing today.

While an epilogue is normally the final word, it is important to me that the *absolute* final word be one more story from a woman with endo, a woman who is the epitome of persistence. In some respects, her case is the most unique I've ever encountered. Unique, because she suffered with endo for forty long years. Unique, because I diagnosed her when she was sixty-three years old. I know, that doesn't seem to make sense in theory. Once you hit menopause in your forties or fifties, your hormone levels decline, so you would expect the endo symptoms to fade. That wasn't the case for Madeleine, which is why her condition was so rare.

But I don't want you to focus on that aspect. How and why that happened to her is a topic for a future book on some of my more complicated cases. I want, instead, for you to digest one more story on how indiscriminate and crafty this disease is. Despite having the resources to receive high-quality medical care, it took forty years for Madeleine to treat endo—and that was only after she diagnosed herself with it. The endo fooled her and doctors over and over and over again.

But in the end, Madeleine found the treatment she needed.

She found treatment because, like every woman in this book, she never stopped listening. She never stopped searching. She never stopped questioning. She never stopped believing. And she never stopped trusting. She'll be the first to say that there was nothing easy or pleasant about her journey toward healing, but she'll also tell you that it was well worth the effort.

My Name Is Madeleine

"Today, I look toward the future rather
than what I lost in the past."

Unlike most of the girls you've read about, I didn't have awful cramps
or debilitating pain when I was young. My problem was specifically
with my bowels. Right before my period, I would become bloated
and constipated, and the day of my period I would get diarrhea. I
just assumed it was all a natural part of having my period.

When I turned twenty-four, my symptoms expanded to include
stomachaches, nausea, abdominal distension, and indigestion. I went
to a doctor who diagnosed me with IBS, known back then as "spas-
tic colon." He told me to take Mylanta and come back in a year.
I believed him and did as he instructed, and why wouldn't I? My
family had access to supposedly the best doctors anywhere. It was
also the first time any doctor had diagnosed me with anything,
and he seemed confident in his conclusion. The word *endometriosis*
wasn't even in my vocabulary.

Unfortunately, Mylanta didn't help, nor did any prescription medication I took in later years, and the symptoms didn't relent. The
worst ones in my twenties and thirties were constipation, frequent
stomachaches, and pain down the right side of my leg. I visited several more doctors whose diagnoses were much of the same, things
like heartburn and gastritis. More than one doctor told me I needed
psychological therapy.

I got married at the age of twenty-eight and had a child when
I was thirty-six. It was a horrible pregnancy with continued symptoms that required me to be medicated throughout. One doctor

told me not to worry. "Your IBS will get better after giving birth," he said. But it got much worse, taking over my life in every respect.

It carried over into my job, where on some days I'd have to lay down on my office floor because it was too uncomfortable to sit in my chair. Every time I would schedule a business meeting with someone, I would warn them that I had a stomach condition and might have to cancel the meeting. Rarely could I make plans with friends. If I did, they knew that there was a good chance I would have to cancel. They were supportive, but it was aggravating for all of us.

I naturally entered menopause earlier than normal, at the age of forty-five, but the pain never subsided. At fifty-five my husband and I divorced. My condition wasn't the reason, but there's no doubt that it put a strain on our marriage. Quite frankly, I think he got tired of hearing about my stomach issues and IBS. I know after thirty years of living with the symptoms, which had worsened with time, *I* was certainly tired of it.

I continued searching for answers, coming up empty at every turn. I didn't just try mainstream doctors. I went to multiple homeopathic doctors, biofeedback doctors, acupuncturists. I recall crying once in a doctor's office in Florida from the pain and frustration of it all. And do you know what he said? "Why are you crying? You've had this for more than thirty years. You shouldn't be so upset about something you've had for so long."

I'd finally found something worse than endo pain: someone telling me that I shouldn't be upset about it.

When I was sixty-three years old, simply by chance, I read an article in the *New York Times* written by Dr. Seckin about endometriosis. Since I'd tried everything else over forty years, I figured an appointment with him couldn't hurt. He was confident that I didn't have IBS since the pain was relegated to the right side of my abdomen and not all over it, but he couldn't be sure I had endo since I was about twenty years into menopause.

I took a chance and had him do surgery; he found twenty-seven lesions on my right side and one on my left side. When I woke up, my pain was completely gone. Now my biggest challenge is trying to adjust to my new life of being able to make travel plans or any other plans without fear of having to cancel them, not having to give a disclaimer to business associates before meeting with them, and simply being able to sit and stand all day without any issues. They are good problems to have.

After my surgery, I wrote a letter to a gastroenterologist I'd had for years and told him what Dr. Seckin found. He responded that he suspected at times that I might have endo, but that my gynecologist should have been the one to pick up on it. His reply confirmed for me what I had suspected: there is a huge disconnect between gastroenterologists and gynecologists. I never knew that endo could cause the issues I'd had, so why would I think to even talk to my gynecologist about it? And why wouldn't a gastroenterologist not think to talk to a gynecologist about it? They should be educated about this, and they should be working in tandem. If it weren't for that gap, it's possible that my endo could have been found when I was in my twenties, not my sixties.

Soon after I sent that letter, Dr. Seckin informed me that that gastroenterologist had referred a patient to him, the first time he'd ever done so. There's so much awareness work to be done, but that's progress.

What I hope you'll learn from my story is that I never stopped. At sixty-three years old I was still trying new doctors. And it wasn't another doctor or friend or anyone else who referred me to Dr. Seckin. It was a newspaper article I'd stumbled across. You never know where your help might come from or when, but you have to keep pushing in order to have a chance to find it. I felt defeated more times than I can count, but I never told myself I was going to quit. Today, I look toward the future rather than what I lost in the past. Sure, I think about it, but I'm not bitter. I'm appreciating the moment, enjoying being healthy and well each day, something I'd never experienced before.

ACKNOWLEDGMENTS

Early detection via awareness and education is the only sure path towards preventing the progression of this disease. For this reason, I must thank every person who speaks out about endometriosis.

In particular, thank you to all the brave women and men who shared their stories that brought this book to life: Lexie, Dilara, Emily, Stephanie, Winnie, Melissa, Ali, Bankes, Tanya, Brandilee, Kim, Rachel, Grace, Nicole, Jenna, Donna, Richard, Mel, Chris, Meg, Amy, Liz, Sophie, Prince, Madeleine, Lynn, Ileana, Eva, Miranda, Amanda, Anna, and Casey.

As an endometriosis surgeon, I could never successfully do what I do without the committed team of knowledgeable and passionate people around me. I've learned the same is true when it comes to writing a book about this disease. Thank you to the countless people who have helped me throughout my career and to those who have helped make this book a reality. Padma Lakshmi, your vision and voice has been critical in combatting this disease. The board and staff at the Endometriosis Foundation of America, your work moves mountains.

Alaia Baldwin Aronow, thank you for speaking about your pain with courage.

Bill Croyle, thank you. Without your work this book would not exist. Jeanne Rebillard, thank you. Karli Goldstein, thank you. Mina, the irreplaceable family writer who helped me with this book, thank you. And my wife, Elif, for your tireless support, encouragement, and unparalleled, eternal friendship—I would not be able to do any of this without you.

Resources

Below are links to more information about endometriosis and the work of the Endometriosis Foundation of America (EndoFound). You can sign up for the EndoFound newsletter to keep updated on the latest news from EndoFound at EndoFound.org.

To learn more about the Seckin Endometriosis Center, visit www.drseckin.com.

Fact Sheets

Endometriosis and Adolescents:
www.endofound.org/member_files/editor_files/outreach_materials /2014/Endometriosis_and_Adolescents_Fact_Sheet_7_25.pdf

Endometriosis and Infertility:
www.endofound.org/member_files/editor_files/outreach_materials /2014/Endometriosis_and_Infertility_Fact_Sheet_7_17.pdf

Endometriosis and Pain Management:
www.endofound.org/member_files/editor_files/outreach_materials /2014/Endometriosis_and_Pain_Management_Fact_Sheet_7_17_14.pdf

Endometriosis Tool Kit Personal Pain Profile/Daily Symptom Tracker:
www.endofound.org/member_files/editor_files/resource_materials /Personal_Pain_Profile.pdf

Endometriosis Screening Tool:
www.endofound.org/member_files/editor_files/resource_materials
/Endometriosis_Screening_Tool.pdf

Endometriosis Assessment Guide (approved for use in New York
City public schools):
www.endofound.org/member_files/editor_files/resource_materials
/Assessment_Guide_NYC_Schools.pdf

Endometriosis Worksheet/Tips for Getting Proper Care:
www.endofound.org/member_files/editor_files/resource_materials
/Endometriosis_Survey_Finding_a_Doctor.pdf

Follow **Endofound**:
Facebook/endofound
Twitter.com/endofound
Instagram.com/endofound@endofound

Follow **Dr. Seckin**:
Facebook.com/drseckin
Twitter.com/drseckin
Instagram.com/drseckinmd@drseckin

Index

addiction
  accusations of drug-seeking, 57,
    115–16
  to opioids and narcotics, 107,
    117–23, 125, 126, 128
adoptees and medical records, 65–66
advocacy
  and empowerment, 71–73
  and endurance, 164–65
  by parents, 135–37, 138–39,
    141–42
  public advocacy, 57, 60, 72, 73,
    75–76, 156–57
  self-advocacy, 16, 34, 40, 71–73,
    164–65
Ali, 67–70, 72
Amanda, 23, 118–19, 148–49
Amy, 150–53
anatomy, female
  described, 4–5
  distortions from endo, 25
Anna, 25–26
appendix
  appendicitis misdiagnosis, 9, 33,
    35, 150
  damage to from endo, 6, 22, 29,
    108
Aronow, Alaia Baldwin, xi–xiv
aunts, asking about family history,
  65–66

Bankes, 73, 74–76, 143, 156–58
belief, See disbelief
bike riding, 90, 94
birth control pill
  personal stories, xii, 29, 38, 58, 67,
    82–83, 92, 97, 99–101, 108, 126,
    150, 161
  recommendations on, 95–98
  side effects from, 96, 100

slowing of endo with, 96, 97–98,
  101
bladder issues, personal stories, 28, 29,
  38, 83, 134
bloating
  and diet, 84
  "endo belly," xii, 38, 39
  and IBS misdiagnosis, 32
blood pressure monitors, 45, 47
bowels
  constipation, 19, 32, 37, 79, 84,
    166
  damage to, 6, 42, 60, 83
  painful bowel movements, 15, 22,
    24, 26
  personal stories, 28–29, 58, 82, 83,
    99, 107, 166
  See also IBS (irritable bowel
    syndrome)
boxing, 94
Brandilee, 92–94
breathing, 46, 88, 90

calming apps, 46
carbon dioxide (CO2) laser surgery,
  laparoscopic low-voltage, 111, 113
Casey, 64
cautery, See electric fulguration laser
  surgery
cervical canal, definition and anatomy,
  5
cervix, definition and anatomy, 6
chocolate cysts, 22, 34, 36
Chris, 144, 145–47
clothing, 43, 46
coaches, 18, 51, 56, 159–63
cold scissors method, See laparoscopic
  deep-excision surgery
complications, 6–7, 15, 22, 24–26,
  97–98

CPSIA information can be obtained
at www.ICGtesting.com
Printed in the USA
LVHW091230240320
650924LV00009BA/82

9 781684 423668